DIGITAL CAMERA

DESIGN GUIDE

PETER AITKEN

Digital Camera Design Guide
Copyright © 1998 by The Coriolis Group, Inc.

The Coriolis Group, Inc.
An International Thomson Publishing Company
14455 N. Hayden Road, Suite 220
Scottsdale, Arizona 85260

602/483-0192
FAX 602/483-0193
http://www.coriolis.com

Printed in the United States of America
ISBN 1-57610-184-3
10 9 8 7 6 5 4 3 2 1

Publisher
Keith Weiskamp

Project Editor
Michelle Stroup

Production Coordinator
April Nielsen

Cover Design
Performance Design

Layout Design
April Nielsen

CORIOLIS GROUP BOOKS
an International Thomson Publishing company I(T)P®

Albany, NY • Belmont, CA • Bonn • Boston • Cincinnati • Detroit • Johannesburg • London • Madrid • Melbourne • Mexico City • New York • Paris • Singapore • Tokyo • Toronto • Washington

ACKNOWLEDGMENTS

This book has only a single author, but in many ways it was a team effort. In particular, my thanks go to Michelle Stroup, Jeff Kellum, Chris Rogers, and Nomi Schalit at the Coriolis Group. I could not have completed this project without the assistance of these four talented and dedicated people.

DEDICATION

I dedicate this book with love to my children,
Benjamin and Claire.

CONTENTS

INTRODUCTION

I have been fascinated by photography since I was a little boy. When I was about 8 years old, my Dad set up a darkroom for me in the damp and dingy cellar of our house. It was really basic—I think my enlarger was World War I surplus—but I didn't know any better. I can't say that I created any masterpieces, but I certainly had a lot of fun. My interest continued through high school, where I was the yearbook photographer. My position gave me license to roam the school with my camera, documenting all of the goings on for posterity. I can remember trying to sneak a picture in the girl's locker room by opening the door a bit, sticking my camera through the crack, and taking a shot "blind." Convinced that I had something really interesting, I rushed to the darkroom to develop the picture only to discover I had a beautiful shot of a row of lockers!

After I finished college and graduate school my interest continued to grow, and I soon decided that I needed to go beyond what I could teach myself from books and magazines. I was fortunate to be able to attend the Ansel Adams Photography Workshop and study with the photographer who is considered to be one of the all-time greats. This experience was a revelation for me, and continues to have a strong influence on my work.

I have been involved with computers for quite a while, almost since the first PC was released. For many years, my interests in computers and in photography were separate. Digital imaging was in its infancy, and there was nothing that a computer could offer in terms of image creation and manipulation that would interest a photographer. The cheapest drugstore print was miles ahead of the most sophisticated computer hardware.

Things have changed. Technology moves at an amazing pace, and over the past few years we have seen digital photography advance to the point where cost and quality are no longer obstacles to creation of high quality images. Many dedicated film photographers are getting involved with digital imaging, and lots of newcomers are taking their first photograph digitally. Who knows—they may never use film at all!

Digital photography is a very flexible tool. If you are to get the most out of it, however, some preparation is required. You need to master not only your digital camera, but also a scanner and a variety of software procedures that you'll use to improve and manipulate your images. That's where this book comes in. I cover all aspects of digital photography, including using your camera and scanner. A series of hands-on projects teaches you how to manipulate your images once they are taken, everything from fixing flaws to changing backgrounds and creating greeting cards. You'll also learn about printing your images and using images on the Web.

I hope that you have as much fun using this book as I did writing it!

Peter G. Aitken
Chapel Hill, North Carolina
August 12, 1997

PART 1

GETTING
THE
PICTURE

Figure 1.1   Digital photography techniques make it easy to convert ordinary pictures like this…

It hasn't been all that long, perhaps 150 years, since the birth of photography. Back then, it seemed like magic. The cumbersome equipment, noxious chemicals, and limited capabilities did not prevent pioneering photographers from creating pictures that thrilled the world. In the years that followed, the technology advanced, cameras got smaller and cheaper, color techniques were developed, and photography as a whole evolved from the province of specialized practitioners to the everyday point-and-shoot convenience that we take for granted today. Until now, one thing has remained static, however: Photography as a chemical process, based on light-sensitive substances coated onto film or paper and developed using chemical baths.

All that is starting to change. The advent of digital photography is likely to have a more profound impact on the field than anything that has come before. No longer is film required to take photographs, and there are no smelly chemicals required for development, and no more expensive trips to the photo lab, either. Photographs are taken electronically and stored in digital form. Once transferred to a computer, the photographs can be manipulated using specialized software programs, transmitted and published electronically, and printed using the personal computer printer that you may already have sitting on your desk.

So, what's the big deal? Anyone who has read *National Geographic* (or any one of a hundred other magazines) knows that traditional photographic techniques are capable of creating the most astounding and beautiful images. How could digital photography possibly be any better? The answer is simple:

- **Cost**. Digital photographs are essentially free. Once you have the necessary equipment, you can take as many photos as you want without additional cost because you do not have to pay for film or processing. You can also experiment freely because unwanted photographs can be erased—making a mistake costs you nothing.

- **Convenience**. In these days of electronic publishing, many photos never need to be printed because their intended use is in an electronic document, such as a Web page. A digital photo is already in the proper format for electronic publishing. There is no need for time-consuming scanning and processing, as is required with traditional photographs.

- **Flexibility**. Digital photography refers not only to photos taken with a digital camera, but it also refers to traditional photographs that have been converted to digital form by scanning (a process we'll cover in Chapter 3). If you have a scanner, digital photography techniques can be applied to your old photos as well as new ones.

- **Creative manipulation**. This is by far the most exciting part of digital photography, and it is in fact the main topic of this book. There is almost no limit to the ways you can change a digital photograph, from correcting flaws to expressing your creative ideas.

Figure 1.2   …to eye-catching images like this.

What will this book teach you? I will present the information and techniques you need to master every aspect of digital photography, from snapping the photo to enjoying the finished product. The book is divided into several sections, as follows:

- The first part, which you're reading now, covers getting the picture. This includes looking at how digital cameras work, discussing photographic techniques, and learning how to scan images into your computer.

- The second part shows you a variety of techniques you can use to correct flaws in your photographs.

- The third section demonstrates the wide range of creative manipulations that let you apply your own personal vision to your photographs.

- The fourth section deals with various end uses for digital photographs, such as printing, desktop publishing, and Web documents.

• The appendix explains the basics of using Paint Shop Pro, which is the main tool you'll be using to work with your photographs (the program is on the CD-ROM enclosed with this book).

How Computers Store Photographs

How can a photograph be stored in a computer? The same way a computer does everything—digitally. You need to understand how a computer stores information before you can understand how it stores photographs.

Computer Data Storage

The basic unit of information storage in a computer is called a *bit*. A single bit can take only two values: 1 or 0. (These are also referred to as on or off, yes or no, and true or false.) In the computer's circuits, a 1 bit is represented by a positive voltage, and a 0 bit is represented by absence of voltage. There are differences in the details sometimes, but the general idea is the same. This is called binary, or digital, information storage. The same principle is at work in the computer's memory, on its disk drives, on a CD-ROM, and in the signals sent over a modem.

A single bit is not very useful, but when you have lots of them, the possibilities become almost endless. Traditionally, computer data storage is divided into a unit called a *byte*. One byte contains 8 bits and can therefore store many different values: 00000000, 00000001, 00000011, and up to 11111111. When you work it out, you'll see that a byte can take 256 different values. Thus, individual bytes are used to store numbers ranging from 0 to 255, as well as typographical characters (letters, punctuation marks, and so on). When more flexibility is needed—for example, to store numbers larger than 255—two or more bytes are strung together. This same storage method is used for all information in a computer, not just for images.

HOW MANY BYTES?

A typical PC will have at least 8 million bytes, or 8 megabytes (MB), of memory and several hundred MB of hard disk storage.

Digital Image Storage

How can an image be represented as bytes for storage in a computer? The answer is quite similar to the way photographs are printed in a newspaper. Look closely at a newspaper photograph and you'll see that it is made up of a grid of dots. Where the photo is dark, the dots are larger, and where the photo is lighter, they are smaller. When viewed at normal distances, the individual dots are not visible but blend together into the final image. You can see this in Figure 1.3.

Figure 1.3 Newspaper photographs are comprised of a series of dots.

Digital photos work in the same manner. When the image is first created, either in a digital camera or on a scanner, it is broken up into a grid of dots, called *pixels* (for *pic*ture *el*ements). For each pixel, the brightness and, for color photographs, the color, are measured and expressed as numbers. These numbers are stored by the computer. When the photo is displayed on your screen or is printed, the numbers are converted into the proper color and intensity of light or ink. This is graphically illustrated in Figure 1.4, which shows a portion of a digital photograph enlarged to show the individual pixels.

Because a computer represents a picture as a series of numbers, manipulating the picture becomes a simple matter. Of course, "simple" is a relative term and some of the manipulations that can be performed, including some of those you'll learn in

this book, are somewhat complex. In the old days of film and darkrooms, however, such manipulations would be very difficult—if not totally impossible!

Image Resolution

If digital photography breaks an image into a grid of pixels, the question that naturally arises is how many pixels will the image have? The number of pixels in a digital photograph is referred to as its *resolution*. Resolution is expressed as the number a pixels across the image and the number of pixels from top to bottom. Thus, an image with 640 pixels horizontally and 480 pixels vertically has a resolution of 640×480.

As with many things in life, image resolution presents a trade-off. From a visual point of view, higher resolution is always better. An image with a resolution of 1280×960 will have twice the sharpness and detail as one with a resolution of 640×480. The higher-resolution image will, however, require four times the storage space, containing 1,228,880 pixels as compared with the lower-resolution image with 307,200 pixels. Most typically, color images require 3 bytes of memory, or disk space for each pixel, so we are talking about a 921,600-byte image file as compared to a

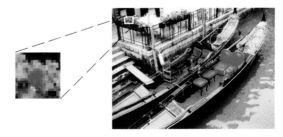

Figure 1.4 In this photograph, an enlarged view of the portion outlined with the white rectangle clearly reveals the individual pixels.

3,686,400-byte file. The larger file takes longer to download from your camera, occupies more disk space, takes longer to load into imaging programs, and takes longer to print.

When creating a digital image, you may or may not have a choice of resolutions. Some digital cameras permit pictures to be taken at only a single resolution, while others offer a choice of two or more resolution settings (sometimes called "standard quality" and "high quality"). Scanners almost always offer a choice of image resolutions.

When you have a choice of resolutions, which should you use? It depends on a number of factors, including the intended use for the photograph. One thing to remember is that cameras that offer a choice can store fewer high-resolution images before requiring a download. For example, my Olympus D-300L can store 120 standard-quality (lower resolution) images but only 30 high-quality images. My choice of resolutions often depends on how soon I will be able to get to my computer and download my images. When scanning images, camera storage is not a concern, but hard disk storage may be—high-resolution images can really eat up disk space. Table 1.1 shows the factors to consider when deciding on what resolution you should use.

Image Color Depth

The other important aspect of digital images is the *color depth*. Color depth refers to the maximum number of different colors that the image can display. Color depth affects not only the appearance of the image, but also the amount of space required to store it.

Table 1.1 Selecting an image resolution.

Prefer lower resolution if ...	Prefer higher resolution if ...
Camera or disk storage capacity is tight	Camera or disk storage capacity is not a concern
The image will be reproduced small	The image will be reproduced large
Visual image quality is not critical	Visual image quality is important
You will be using the entire image	You will be cropping the image

In digital photography, you will almost always be working with one of the following:

- **True color**. The image can display over 16 million different colors (16,777,216 colors to be exact). This mode is called *true color* because it permits images to display realistic, lifelike colors. It requires 3 bytes of storage per pixel.

- **256 color**. The image can display 256 different colors. The range of colors available is the same as for true color mode, but only 256 of the colors can be displayed in the image at one time. 256-color images are rarely used for digital photographs because of the limited number of colors. It requires 1 byte of storage per pixel.

- **Gray scale**. The image has no color but is like a black-and-white photograph, displaying black, white, and grays. There are 256 shades of gray that can be displayed at once. It requires 1 byte of storage per pixel.

To my knowledge, all digital cameras produce true-color images. This makes perfect sense, of course, as you want to create realistic looking pictures of the real world. Why, then, do you need to know about these difference color depths? First of all, you can change the color depth of a photograph after it is taken, and for some special purposes this is desirable or necessary. Second, scanners usually permit you to select the color depth of your scanned images, so you'll need this information when we get to the chapter on scanning.

How Digital Cameras Work

In many ways, digital cameras are similar to the regular film camera that you are used to using. They have a viewfinder that you look through to frame your picture, a button you press to take the picture, and a flash that goes off when the scene is too dark. Inside, however, things are a lot different.

In place of film, a digital camera has a *charge-coupled device*, or CCD. The CCD is a special kind of chip (integrated circuit) that has on its surface a grid of thousands of small units called *wells*. The entire chip is smaller than your thumbnail, so each well is microscopic in size. What is special about a CCD is that each well is sensitive to light. When light falls on the CCD, each individual well responds to the light by building up an electrical charge—the brighter the light, or the longer it shines on the CCD, the more powerful the charge. By using color filters, the wells can be made sensitive to the color of the light as well as the light's intensity.

When you take a picture, the camera shutter opens for a fraction of a second and the camera lens focuses an image of whatever it is pointing at on the CCD. Each well builds up a charge whose strength depends on the color and strength of the light falling on it. After the shutter closes, circuits in the camera read the charge in each well and convert it to a numerical value that is stored digitally. (It is this process that causes the short delay after each picture you take.) Once this process is complete, the charges on the wells are erased and the camera is ready to take another picture.

You may have guessed by now that each well on the CCD corresponds to a pixel in the final image. Thus, my Olympus D-300L creates images of 1024×768 pixels, so we know that the CCD contains a grid of 1024×768 wells. Cameras that offer two resolutions will create the lower-resolution

256-COLOR MODE

Images with 256-color depth are not as limited
as you might think. This is because the 256 colors
in a particular image can be chosen from a selection of over 16 million colors. The exact 256 colors
used in a particular image are referred to as the
image's *palette*. In a photo of a forest glade, for
example, the palette would likely consist mostly
of varying shades of green and brown, and the
resulting image would be reasonably lifelike.
Likewise, a photo of a brilliant sunset would use
a palette containing a variety of reds and oranges.
Figures 1.5 and 1.6 illustrate the difference
between true color and 256 color. The difference
may seem subtle, but will be more obvious on
screen.

Figure 1.5   This true color image uses a
total of 198,037 different colors (determined with Paint Shop Pro's Count Colors
Used command).

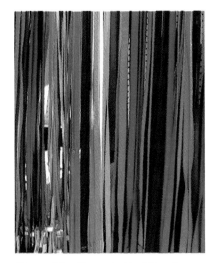

Figure 1.6   Converted to 256-color
mode, the same image looks reasonably
good but there is a noticeable loss of
subtlety and detail.

image by combining the signals from adjacent wells on the CCD to create a single pixel. For example, the Olympus D-300L will average the signals from each 2×2 block of wells to create each pixel in its lower resolution of 512×384 pixels.

Image Storage And Transfer

All digital cameras store photographs digitally, and all have the capability to transfer digital images to a computer. While the principle is the same, the details differ from one type of digital camera to another. Let's take a look at the different types of digital cameras:

- **Direct transfer cameras**. These do not provide any internal image storage. Each image is transferred to a computer as soon as it is taken. Because such cameras are tied to their computer hosts by the interface cable, they are obviously limited to studio work.

- **Internal memory cameras**. These contain their own memory for storage of multiple images. The camera can be connected to your computer via a cable, and the pictures are downloaded onto your hard disk. Once this is done, the camera's memory can be cleared to make room for more photographs.

- **Memory card cameras**. These are similar to internal memory cameras except that some or all of their memory is located in small modules, or cards, that are plugged into a slot on the camera. Images are transferred to the computer either by cable or by removing the memory card from the camera and plugging it into a slot on your computer. In a few models, the card contains a miniature hard disk rather than memory, but the principle remains the same.

DIRECT PRINTING

A few digital cameras offer the option of connecting the camera directly to a special-purpose printer and printing images directly. The method is limited because it does not permit any image manipulation.

Creating Your Original Photographs

No matter how skillful you become at digitally manipulating your images, the quality of your final photos will always depend in large part on the quality of your original images, the ones that come out of your camera. In other words, your skill with the camera will combine with your skill at the computer. Most of this book deals with the second part of this process—what you can do to improve and modify existing photographs. This book is not intended to be a photography course in the sense of teaching you how to take pictures, but I think it's worth going over a few of the basics so you will at least have some awareness of the various things that contribute to a good photograph (and a bad one!).

Subject

Subject matter is perhaps the most important part of any photograph, and it is also the most personal. I certainly cannot advise you what you should take pictures of. Whether it's mountains in Nepal, flowers in a garden, or your 2-year-old daughter with spaghetti in her hair, you must decide what's going to be in your photos. Sometimes the subject matter will be dictated by the job at hand, other times it will be a purely personal choice.

Composition

The term *composition* refers to the way things are arranged in a photograph. You will almost always have some control over the composition of your photos. Sometimes you will be able to actually change the arrangement of the objects. When setting up a family portrait, for example, you could ask people to change their positions. More often, you will exert control over composition by changing the point of view from which the photo is taken. There are several ways to do this:

- Aim the camera differently to change the framing. Without changing your position, you can sometimes dramatically improve a photograph simply by pointing the camera a little bit up, down, left, or right. Most people have the natural tendency to center the subject in the photograph, but this does not always provide the best results.

- Move closer to or farther away from the subject. If your camera has a zoom lens, you can accomplish the same thing by zooming in or out. Digital manipulation lets you "move closer" after the fact by cropping the photograph on your computer, but the resulting image is always of lower quality than the original, because a cropped photograph always has lower resolution (fewer pixels) than the original. Whenever possible, crop "in the camera" to obtain the best quality images.

- Move to the left or to the right. This may provide a better angle on the subject, and can also bring a more attractive background into view.

- Move higher or lower. Often your options in this area are limited, but you can always crouch down or hold your camera over your head.

- Turn your camera. Almost all cameras take rectangular photographs, and the simple act of turning the camera to take a vertical rather than a horizontal photo can often result in significant improvement.

SO, WHAT'S CROPPING?

Cropping an image means to trim one or more of its edges so that only the central portion remains.

THE CLOSER THE BETTER

If I could give just one piece of advice to aspiring photographers, it would be "get closer." In many of the photographs I see, the main subject takes up a small portion of the image and the remainder is foreground, background, sky—stuff not related to the main subject. Closer is not always better, of course. In some photos, the surroundings are an important part of the picture, like when you snap your kids standing in front of Mount Rushmore. Often, however, moving closer to your subject can be the easiest and surest way to turn a good photograph into a better one.

Figure 1.7 This photograph's composition leaves a lot to be desired.

Figure 1.7 is an example of a photograph with poor composition. The main subject—the train—occupies only a small part of the photograph. There is too much uninteresting foreground and blank sky. What's more, the bright clothing on some of the people at the left side of the tracks is distracting. There's lots of room for improvement.

Figure 1.8 shows a photo of the same subject that I took a few seconds later. I think you'll agree that it is much improved. I used three of the techniques listed earlier, as follows:

1. I moved closer to the subject (in this case, the subject was also moving closer to me).

2. I turned the camera to take a vertical photograph.

3. I aimed the camera higher to avoid including too much empty foreground in the photograph.

Figure 1.8 Thanks to improved composition, the second photograph of the train is more dramatic.

Background

A photograph's background is related to the overall composition, of course, but background is so important in itself that I gave it its own section. True, not all photographs have a background—a shot of mountains in the distance or a beautiful sunset are two examples. Most photos do have backgrounds, however, defined as whatever you see in the photo behind the main subject. The background can make or break a photograph, so you need to pay attention to it.

Perhaps the main reason that so many photos seem to have background problems is that the photographer was (naturally enough) paying attention to the main subject. If you are totally engrossed in trying to get your dog to stand still for a photo, you may not notice that a garbage truck has just pulled into the background. A little bit of attention to what's behind the subject can have a big impact on your photographs.

Lighting

Without light, there cannot be photographs. The quality of the light can have a huge impact on how a photo comes out. After all, the light can make a difference in our daily lives. When you're having a romantic dinner with your sweetie, would you prefer overhead fluorescent lights, or perhaps would a candle be better? A rather dramatic example, but you get the idea.

There's a better reason to attend to the lighting other than mere mood. The human eye is a much more sophisticated device than any camera, and is much better at seeing details in bright and dark areas. Imagine for a moment an outdoor sunlit scene that includes some dark shadows. Your eye will be able to make out the details in both the brightest areas of the scene as well as the dark shadows. Cameras and imaging techniques (at least the kind that you'll be using for your digital photographs) do not have this ability, and cannot capture details in both very bright and very dark areas in the same picture. A scene that looked great when you saw it may not look so good in the photograph.

IT'S FREE!

Remember that digital photos are free—there's no cost for film or developing. You can experiment with different lighting as much as you want until you get it right.

Figure 1.9 shows an example of how a change in lighting can improve a photograph. I photographed my wife, Maxine, in direct overhead sunlight (top), and then took another shot in open shade under some trees (bottom). I don't think there's any doubt which is the better photo.

Of course, you may not be able to do anything about the lighting in many of your photographs. That's fine, but when you do have some control, you should be aware of the difference it can make. Direct overhead sunlight is a tough situation, and you may have to live with it, unless you can move your subject or can come back later when the sun is lower or on an overcast day. Slanting sunlight is easier to work with, and a slightly overcast day often results in the best photographs. Of course. I am talking about my personal preferences—you may like the harsh shadows that sunlight creates.

Summing Up

Digital techniques bring a wide range of exciting possibilities to photography. With camera technology improving (and prices falling), this exciting field is open to almost everyone. Whether you are interested in personal artistic expression, recording family activities, or creating images for commercial and Internet use, digital photography gives you power and flexibility that simply were not available a few years ago.

Figure 1.9 Lighting can make a major difference in how your pictures come out.

USING YOUR
DIGITAL 2
CAMERA

Taking good photographs is not as easy as some think. If you've done any photography, you probably know what I'm talking about. Photos that seemed great when you took them often turn out...well, a bit disappointing. Don't worry, you're not alone. Every photographer, even the seasoned pro, has a lot of shots that don't turn out as planned. Your goal should not be to have every photo come out great, because that's not going to happen. Rather, you should work on gradually improving your success rate.

How do you go about improving your photographs? The way I see it, there are three parts to this process. First, you need to be familiar and comfortable with your camera. Second, you should be able to apply basic principles of photography. And finally, you must practice, practice, practice. In this chapter, I will help you with the first and second parts, but the practicing is up to you.

Camera Basics

Digital cameras come in many different models, and while the details may differ from camera to camera, there are still many things that all cameras have in common. Some of the features and controls you'll find on digital cameras are also present on standard film cameras. Other aspects of digital cameras are unique and are not found on film cameras.

Exposure

The term *exposure* refers to the amount of light required to record a photograph. Exposure is controlled primarily by the camera's shutter. When you take a photo, the shutter opens briefly and allows light to fall on the charge-coupled device, or CCD (described in Chapter 1). The CCD has a certain built-in sensitivity to light; if there is not enough light the resulting photograph will be dark, and if there is too much light the photo will be excessively bright. If you are photographing a bright scene, the shutter needs to open for only a short period to

LOOK, THINK, LOOK AGAIN

The most important thing you can do to improve your pictures is to figure out what's wrong (or right) with them. That's where the phrase "look, think, look again" comes from: *look* at a photograph, *think* about what makes it a good photograph (or a disappointing one), then *look* at it again and consider what you might do differently the next time. This does not apply only to your own photos; when you see a photograph that really strikes you in this or another book, or in a magazine, look at it and try to figure out what makes the photograph special. Is it the color? The composition? The lighting? Learn by looking, that's what I say.

admit enough light. If the scene is dim, the shutter must remain open for a longer time. Of course, even a "long" exposure time is pretty brief by human standards, perhaps being one-eighth of a second. A short exposure will be on the order of one five-hundredth of a second. Figures 2.1 through 2.3 illustrate the effects improper exposure can have on a photograph.

Exposure is also controlled by the camera's *aperture*. You can think of the aperture as the hole through which the light passes. If the aperture is wide, then more light will pass while the shutter is open. If the aperture is small, less light will pass through the shutter.

A good analogy would be water flowing through a faucet. The amount of water that comes out of the faucet corresponds to the amount of light that hits the camera's CCD. The amount of water is controlled by both the amount of time the faucet is open (like the shutter in your camera) and by how wide it is opened (the aperture).

Most modern cameras have automatic exposure, meaning that the camera senses the amount of light present and sets the exposure time and aperture accordingly. Automatic systems are very convenient, permitting you to concentrate on your

Figure 2.1 Colors are bright and vibrant in a properly exposed photograph.

Figure 2.3 Too much exposure results in faded and washed-out colors.

Figure 2.2 Underexposure results in a dark photograph with muddy colors.

subject rather than on the technical details of your camera. In most picture-taking situations, the automatic exposure systems do a wonderful job. They are not perfect, however, and under some conditions they can be fooled. If you are aware of these situations, you can take steps to prevent an improperly exposed photograph.

Exposure problems occur most often when the main subject is a lot brighter or darker than the background. A good example is photographing people under an umbrella on a sunny beach. The people are shaded, but the camera's automatic exposure system sees mostly the bright sky and sand. The exposure is set accordingly, and in the resulting photograph, the people under the umbrella are too dark. A similar situation can occur when photographing a bright subject against a dark background, only the results are opposite—the subject is too bright.

What can you do in these situations? The most direct method is simply to get closer to your subject. If the subject is "bigger," taking up more of the image area, the camera's automatic exposure system will see more of the dark subject and less of the bright background, and the exposure will be set more accurately.

Sometimes you will not be able to get closer to your subject (or even if you can, you may not want to). In such situations, you may be able to take advantage of your camera's exposure lock feature, if it is available. Not all cameras offer exposure lock— you'll have to check your instruction manual to see if it has this feature. Here's how exposure lock works:

1. Point the camera at something that has brightness similar to your intended subject, but without a bright background.

2. Depress the shutter button slightly to lock in the exposure setting.

3. While keeping the shutter button partially depressed, frame your subject within the viewfinder.

4. Press the shutter button completely to take the photo.

CENTER WEIGHTING

Most automatic exposure systems are center-weighted. Center weighting means that more emphasis is placed on the light levels in the center of the image than light levels at the edges.

The last possible solution to this kind of exposure problem is to use your camera's exposure compensation control. An exposure compensation control lets you override the camera's automatic exposure, either brightening or darkening the photo by a set amount. With a little experience, you will learn to judge which photos require compensation. This feature is currently not available on digital cameras, but I expect it to be soon, hopefully by the time you read this book.

Focus

Just like your eyes, a camera must be focussed on the subject if the image is to be sharp. If you focus on something close up, distant objects will be blurry, and vice versa. Focussing is automatic in most digital cameras, but just like the automatic exposure system, the auto focus system can be fooled.

Auto focus works by examining a small part of the image and changing the focus until the details are sharp. This is why there is usually a brief delay between pressing the shutter button and the picture actually being taken—the camera is focussing. The region of the image where the focus is measured is usually marked in the viewfinder by a box or crosshairs; it is almost always directly in the center of the image.

Problems can arise if your subject is off-center. The camera will focus on the background and the main subject may be blurry, illustrated by Figure 2.4. You can deal with this by using the camera's focus lock, which operates in a manner similar to the exposure lock discussed in the previous section. Center the subject in the viewfinder and press the shutter button part way to lock the focus. Then, reframe the picture as desired and depress the shutter button all the way to take the

Figure 2.4   With the main subject off-center, the camera focussed on the background and the intended subject is blurred.

picture. Take a look at the same picture made using this technique (Figure 2.5).

There are other ways an auto focus system can be fooled. If there is something between you and your subject, for example, when taking a picture through a fence, the camera may focus on the closer object instead of on the subject. Problems can also arise if the central area of the image does not contain any details. With nothing to focus on, the auto focus system cannot operate. Because there are different kinds of auto focus systems, the specifics of how they work, how they can be fooled, and what you can do about it, will differ from camera to camera. Look in your camera's instruction manual for the details on how yours works.

Figure 2.5 By locking the focus on the main subject, then reframing the image, the proper focus is obtained.

Special Techniques

Many of the photographs you take will be straightforward—frame the subject and push the shutter button. That's the beauty of automatic cameras—they let you concentrate on your photograph without worrying about camera setting. At times, however, you'll come across special situations in which your camera's automatic capabilities are not enough.

Flash

Most digital cameras are equipped with a flash. This can be an extremely useful accessory, permitting you to take photographs in situations where the lighting would otherwise be too dark. A flash can also improve photographs where the lighting conditions are not ideal. Your camera probably has several different flash settings, and you need to know how to use them in order to make the best use of your flash. Not all cameras offer the complete range of flash settings, and some may offer additional flash

SHUTTER SPEED AND BLURRED PHOTOS

If either the subject or the camera is moving when a photo is taken, you run the risk of a blurry photograph. This problem most often occurs when working in dim light, because relatively slow shutter speeds will be required. To minimize camera movement, hold your camera steadily with both hands and *squeeze* the shutter button rather than jabbing it quickly. Jabbing the shutter button is likely to cause the camera to shake. You can sometimes compensate for subject movement by *panning* the camera, moving it to keep the moving subject centered in the viewfinder. The background may be blurred, but the subject—for example, a running horse—will not be.

flexibility. You will need to read your camera's instruction manual for details on the camera's flash settings and how to use them. Following are some of the more common flash modes:

- **Normal.** This flash mode is usually the camera's default setting—the setting that will be in effect without any special actions on your part. In normal mode, the flash goes off only when the camera's automatic exposure system detects that there is not enough existing, or ambient, light to take the photo.

- **Fill-in.** This flash mode causes the flash to fire regardless of the light level. You may wonder what the point is of firing the flash when photographing, for example, a sunny outdoor scene. Such brightly lit scenes often have dark shadows that detract from the photograph. For instance, a person wearing a hat may have a shadowed face that makes it impossible to tell whether it is Aunt Emily or Uncle Ned. The fill-in flash provides enough extra light to fill in the shadows so that they are not so dark in the final photograph. I find the fill-in flash to be particularly useful when photographing people outdoors in the sun.

- **Red-eye reduction.** This mode can prevent the annoying "red eye" that you sometimes see in flash photographs of people looking directly at the camera. Red eye is caused by light from the flash entering the subject's eye and reflecting back to the camera. The reflected light is red because of blood vessels in the eye. The result is a bright red spot in the center of each eye,

making the person look a bit demonic. Red-eye reduction mode works by firing the flash at low power a few times immediately before the photo is taken. Assuming the subject is looking at the camera, this causes the pupils to contract. Thus, when the flash fires at full power for the actual photograph, there is less chance of light entering the eye and reflecting back.

- **Flash off.** This mode prevents the flash from firing no matter how dark the scene you are photographing. Use this flash mode to preserve the natural light mood in a scene where the flash would normally fire.

Macro Photography

The term *macro photography* refers to extreme close-ups. Macro photography can be very useful, whether you are documenting an industrial process, photographing an electrical component, or simply capturing the beauty of a flower, like the example in Figure 2.6.

Photo courtesy of Maxine Okazaki

Figure 2.6 The beauty and intricacy of this Cattleya orchid is best captured with macro photography.

FIXED FOCUS

Some of the less expensive digital cameras use what is called a *fixed focus* lens. There is no auto focus, and, in fact, no focussing adjustments of any kind. The camera is designed so that everything from four to five feet and farther from the camera is always in focus. Using fixed focus cameras has one obvious advantage: You don't need to worry about proper focussing. However, these cameras cannot take photos of anything close, and they are generally not suited for taking pictures in low-light situations.

There is no strict dividing line where macro photography begins and regular photography ends, but if you are within one foot or less from your subject, you know you have entered the realm of macro photography. Your ability to take macro photographs depends on your camera: Some digital cameras do not have macro capability, limiting you to subjects that are at least three or four feet away. Others achieve macro capability by means of a special accessory lens that clips over the camera's main lens for close focussing. Still others have a special setting for macro photography, requiring no special accessories.

However your camera works, there is one special consideration to keep in mind: *depth of focus*. This term refers to the range of distances within which things are in proper focus. When working at normal distances, depth of focus is rarely a concern. If you are photographing a group of people, for example, you may focus on someone 10 feet away, but people 7 feet away and people 20 feet away will also be in focus. With close-up photography, however, the depth of focus is much more restricted. If you are photographing a printed circuit board for your company's sales brochure, you may find that while the front edge of the board is in good focus, the back edge is blurry because the depth of focus did not extend that far. The statuettes in Figure 2.7 illustrate this. The camera was focussed on the third statuette (which you'll notice is sharp), but the ones in front of and behind it are out of focus.

Figure 2.7 Depth of focus is limited in macro photography.

Restricted depth of focus in macro photography is not a flaw of your camera design, but rather a fundamental principle of optics. You cannot change it, but you can learn to work around some of its limitations. Here are some suggestions:

- Arrange your subject to decrease the range of distances that need to be in focus. In the circuit board example given earlier, you might change the position of the circuit board so it is not at such a sharp angle.

- Increase the illumination. Providing brighter light will allow your camera to use a smaller aperture. With smaller apertures, depth of focus is increased.

- Move farther away from the subject. The closer you are, the more restricted depth of focus you have. By moving back and then later cropping the photograph digitally, you may be able to obtain the desired results without losing too much image quality.

Still Life Photography

The term *still life* may make you think of a painting of a wine bottle and fruit, but the term really means any photograph of small- to moderate-sized inanimate objects. Taking a photo of an electronic banana peeler for your company's catalog? That's a still life. Snapping a shot of your ceramic golf clubs to post on a Web auction? That's a still life too. Who knows, maybe the artist in you wants to photograph a wine bottle with fruit. In any case, still life photography is not all that difficult once you know the basics.

Perhaps the most important thing to pay attention to when taking a still life photo is the background. You want the item being photographed to stand out, without anything in the photo that might distract the viewer. You need a *seamless* background, so called because there are no visible seams or edges. You can make your own seamless background quite easily. You'll need a piece of heavy paper or thin cardboard of the appropriate size; try a hobby shop if you don't have anything on hand. (The color is up to you.) Move a table against a wall. Above the table a distance of about half the size of the paper, tape one edge of the paper against the wall. Thus, if your paper is four feet long, you would tape it to the wall two feet above the table. Attach the other end of the paper to the table top approximately the same distance from the wall. Do not fold the paper—where it bends from the vertical wall to the horizontal table, you want a smooth curve. Figure 2.8 illustrates the arrangement.

Place the object being photographed on the paper. When you frame the shot, the background will be only the paper, smooth and seamless. For really large items, you can skip the table and use the floor. It can be difficult to find paper large enough for large photographic objects; a photographic specialty store may be your best bet. But don't use a bed sheet or similar item. In my experience, it is impossible to hide the wrinkles, and your shots always look like you used a sheet for a backdrop—very amateurish!

The next requirement is lighting. In almost all cases, still life photography is done with artificial light rather than natural light (like the sun shining through a window) because it is completely under your control. You can achieve very good results with only two lights, and they don't have to be fancy. Your standard household reading lamps

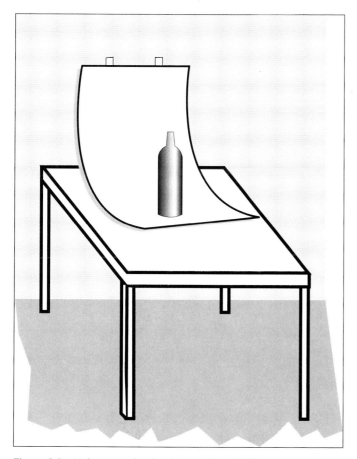

Figure 2.8 Make a seamless background for still life photographs.

are just fine, although you may want to remove the shades. Position one light on each side of the camera and adjust them to get the desired lighting effects. Proper lighting depends on the subject, of course, but two general rules for still life photography are as follows:

- You do not want harsh shadows, but subtle shadows may be desirable. By positioning one of the two lamps closer, or making it brighter, you can obtain gentle shadows that help add a three-dimensional quality to the photograph.

- Avoid large reflections. This is a problem only if the item being photographed has a shiny surface. If you see such reflections through your camera's viewfinder, change the position of the lights or of the subject slightly to get rid of them.

NO FLASH

Avoid the temptation to use your camera's built-in flash for still life shots. Such direct and harsh lighting almost always produces inferior results. With flash, it is impossible to obtain the subtle shadows that are possible with a dual-light system. The probability of reflections is greatly increased too. Most important, flash does not permit you to view the lighting effects before taking the photograph.

Finally, you should have a tripod. While not an absolute requirement, mounting your camera on a tripod makes it easier to precisely frame the picture and also prevents blur due to camera shake.

Copying Documents

If you do not have a scanner, it may be possible to use your digital camera to make copies of documents. I am not talking about straight photocopies of newspaper articles and the like, but rather copies of old family photos, color magazine pages, and basically anything that is flat—even your mom's "Home Sweet Home" cross-stitch. Once you've made a digital copy of something, you can store it, email it, print it out, and so on.

Copying documents is like still life photography in some ways, but the fact that the subject is flat introduces certain difficulties. It is essential, of course, that the image be sharply focussed over the entire document—one or two blurry corners may render the copy unusable. To ensure a completely sharp image, it is necessary that the back of your camera be parallel to the original document. This is next to impossible to achieve with a hand-held camera, so it is strongly advised that you use a tripod for document copying. Then there are two basic ways to work:

- Place the document on a flat surface, such as the floor or a table. Do not cover it with glass, as you will likely get reflections. Position the camera on the tripod above the document, looking down at it. Use a small carpenter's level to ensure that both the document and the camera are level, measuring front-to-back as well as left-to-right.

- Tape or tack the document to a vertical surface, like a wall. Position the camera on the tripod in front of the document and make sure the camera is centered both left-to-right and top-to-bottom with respect to the document. Use a level to set the camera's back to vertical.

Your next task is to arrange the lighting. For good results, when copying a document, illumination should be even over the entire surface. This is difficult to do without using at least two lights. (You can use almost any kind of lamp as long as the light that it casts is wide enough to cover the entire document.) Position the two lights symmetrically, one on either side of the document. An old pro's trick to check for even illumination is to hold a pencil perpendicular to the document near its center. The pencil will cast two shadows, one from each of the lamps. If the two shadows look equally dark, then your illumination is even.

Summing Up

Whether you are using a digital camera or a film camera, there's a lot to be learned about photography. Certain fundamentals apply equally to either type of camera. To increase your skill as a photographer, you need to know your camera inside and out— how the controls work, what the camera's capabilities are, and so on. You also need to know some of the basics of photography. I've provided an introduction in this chapter, and you can find plenty of additional information at the local library or bookstore. And remember: practice. The best teacher is experience, so get out there and take photos.

SCANNING
YO3UR
IMAGES

The world of digital photography goes far beyond images taken with a digital camera. With a scanner, you can digitize existing images: anything from a regular snapshot taken with a film camera to that antique portrait of your great grandparents' wedding. Once a photograph has been translated into digital form, you can manipulate it as you would a photo that was originally taken with a digital camera. Whether the image was taken with a digital camera or digitized with a scanner makes little or no difference.

Scanning is not a simple matter of slapping the original on your scanner and clicking the Scan button. For the best results, you need to understand how your scanner works, what software settings are available, and how to use the proper scanner settings to get the desired results based on the type of original and the image's intended use. That's what this chapter will teach you.

How Scanners Work

Scanners and digital cameras operate on similar principles. An image of the original is projected onto an array of light-sensitive elements that convert the brightness and color of the light into a voltage. The voltage, in turn, is converted to a digital value. The resulting digital values are combined to create the pixels of the final digital image. The primary difference between a digital camera and a scanner is that a camera "captures" the entire image at once by using a rectangular array of light-sensitive elements, while a scanner captures the image a row at a time by scanning the image with a single line of light-sensitive elements.

Types Of Scanners

Scanners come in a variety of configurations. The type you should consider depends on both your planned scanning needs and your budget.

- **Drum scanners**. This type of scanner provides the highest level of image quality. They are typically found at professional printing businesses. In a drum scanner, the original is attached to a cylindrical drum and rotated past the sensing elements. These scanners are very expensive, with capabilities that go well beyond the needs of desktop scanning.

- **Flatbed scanners**. This type of scanner provides a flat glass surface onto which the original is placed. The illumination and sensing elements move under the glass to scan the image. Flatbed scanners are available in a wide range of sizes, prices, and capabilities.

- **Single sheet scanners**. This type of scanner is designed for single sheets of paper. You insert one edge of the paper in a slot and the scanner grabs it, feeds it past the sensing array, and passes it out the other side. Some single sheet scanners are even integrated into keyboards.

- **Photo scanners**. This type of scanner is designed to scan snapshots up to approximately 4×6 inches in size. Some are separate desktop units, others install directly into a computer— much like a diskette drive.

- **Hand scanners**. This type of scanner requires the user to manually scan an image. Hand scanners look something like an overgrown mouse. To scan, you manually drag the unit over the original document.

- **Slide scanners**. This type of scanner is designed for scanning slides (transparencies) rather than opaque originals, such as photographic prints.

Scanner Capabilities

Separate from the type of scanner are its capabilities, or specifications, which are important in determining the quality of the scans. As you might expect, scanners with better specifications cost more. The good news is that you can get a scanner with very good specs for a very reasonable price. Scanner specs fall into two categories: color depth and resolution.

Color Depth

Color depth determines the number of different colors the scanner can record. Essentially, every scanner sold today offers a color depth of at least 8 bits per color, sometimes specified as an overall color depth of 24 bits (8 bits for each of the three primary colors). This means that the scanner can differentiate 2^8, or 256, different levels of each primary color—red, blue, and green. Because digital image files also use 8 bits (one byte) per color for each pixel, this works out perfectly.

Some higher-end scanners offer color depths of 10 or even 12 bits per color, meaning that 1,024 or 4,096 different color levels can be detected for each primary. This does not mean that your final digital image file will contain all of this information because, as mentioned before, the files are limited to 8 bits per color. Rather, the scanner hardware and/or software will process the 10 or 12 bits of color information to generate an 8-bit value that will be more accurate than if the scanner had only 8 bits of information to start with. Scanners with higher color depths still create 8-bit-per-color files, but they tend to produce superior results with originals that have a greater difference between light and dark areas (known as a large dynamic range).

Resolution

The other scanner spec you need to be aware of is *resolution* (dots per inch, or dpi). Because scans have two dimensions—height and width—the resolution of a scanner is expressed as two values, pixels per inch horizontally and pixels per inch vertically. Strangely enough, these values are not always the same for a given scanner, so you will see resolution specs such as 600×300.

You can use a scanner at a lower resolution than its specification, but you cannot go higher. Evaluating a scanner's resolution spec is easy—higher is always better. Higher resolution is also more expensive, and it's pointless to pay for capabilities you won't use. Typical resolution specs are 300×600 or 600×600, with values as high as 1900×3800 in slide scanners where the small size of the original necessitates high resolutions. The reason is that slide images are almost always enlarged for printing or display, and enlargement reduces the effective resolution. If a 1-inch-wide slide is scanned at 1,200 dpi and then printed at a width of 8 inches, the final resolution is reduced by a factor of 8 to 150 dpi, which is barely adequate.

It is essential that you look at a scanner's *optical resolution* and not its *interpolated resolution*. Optical resolution refers to the actual capabilities of the scanner hardware. A scanner's optical resolution is the most important factor in determining the quality of your scans. Interpolated resolution is a software trick that generates additional pixels by averaging adjacent "real" pixels. For example, if the original image has a black pixel next to a white pixel, the interpolation process would generate a gray pixel between them. Interpolation does not add detail to an image, and instead tends to soften the image, making it appear less sharp. Who is to say that between the black pixel and the white pixel there shouldn't be a red pixel instead of the gray pixel that the interpolation process inserted there? Adding pixels by way of interpolation has its uses at times, but be sure that you take into account a scanner's true optical resolution when making a purchase decision.

Selecting A Scanner

If you are considering buying a scanner, you'll find some suggestions in this section helpful when making your decision. The most important question to ask yourself is, what will I be scanning? Will your scanning needs be limited to snapshots, or will you want to scan large photographs and full sheets of paper? Are you happy scanning only single sheets, or do you need the capability to scan bound magazines and books as well? How about scanning slides—never, occasionally, or often? One important factor that I cannot help you with is your budget! Otherwise, however, here are some things to think about. Note that I omit drum scanners from this discussion—they are a high-end item, and are rarely if ever seen attached to a personal computer.

- Handheld scanners are suitable only for small originals that are no wider than the scanner itself. In theory, most hand scanners permit you to scan a wide original in two or more passes and "stitch" the scans together into a final image. This, however, never works as well as the manufacturers claim. If you have a steady hand, you can get decent results with a hand scanner on snapshots and similar originals, but I suggest you consider this type of scanner only as a last resort.

- Single sheet scanners were originally designed for digitizing documents and images for archiving and *optical character recognition*, the conversion of printed text into computer files. These inexpensive scanners' optical resolution and component quality make them less than ideal for scanning images that will be used for digital manipulation of the sort covered in this book. You can produce reasonable images with a single sheet scanner, but I do not recommend buying one specifically for this kind of work.

- Photo scanners are designed specifically to scan photographs, and they provide very good results. If you can live with their limitations as far as the size of originals that can be scanned, then this type of scanner may be a good choice for you.

- Flatbed scanners are by far the most flexible type of scanner available. They can accept almost any type of original, from a wallet-sized photograph to a bound book. Flatbed scanners are also available in a wide range of sizes and specifications, so you are almost sure to find one that fits your needs and budget. Many flatbed scanners offer an optional transparency adapter, which provides additional flexibility, although the results you get from scanning typical slides (from a 35mm camera) are not as good as what you would get using a dedicated slide scanner.

- Slide scanners are dedicated to scanning transparencies. Most of the ones I have seen are limited to 35mm slides. Because the originals are so small, slide scanners need very high optical resolution, with values on the order of 2,000 dots per inch, and higher values are not uncommon. This high resolution is what makes a dedicated slide scanner superior to a flatbed scanner with a transparency adapter for scanning slides.

For most general purpose scanning, a flatbed scanner is the best choice. As for resolution, I recommend 600×600 optical resolution. If your images will be printed only at small sizes, or will be used solely for on-screen display, you can probably get by with 300×300. If you will be scanning a lot of slides, you may want to consider a dedicated slide scanner.

When choosing a scanner, remember that technical advances come quickly. By the time you read this, new models and types of scanners will almost surely be available. For example, Hewlett-Packard is planning to introduce a small photo scanner that has the capability to scan both snapshots and slides.

Scanning Techniques

Scanning software comes in many shapes and sizes. Some programs try to make the scanning process as simple as possible, automating portions of the task and making assumptions about scanner settings. Other programs permit a lot of manual intervention, obliging the user to make decisions about settings such as resolution and color depth. Automatic settings often work quite well, but I feel strongly that you are always better off if you do it yourself. After all, software that permits manual settings will also have an automatic option, so if you understand scanner settings and how to choose them for the best results, then you can rely on automatic settings when and if they provide the desired results.

Because every scanner comes with its own software, I cannot provide instructions on using your specific scanning program. I can, however, explain some of the fundamentals of scanning and leave you to figure out how things are implemented in your scanning program.

The Twain Interface

Most graphics programs, including the Paint Shop Pro program included on the CD-ROM supplied with this book, use the TWAIN interface to acquire images from scanners. When you create the scan, the resulting image is transferred directly to Paint Shop Pro without the need for an intermediate file. You then use Paint Shop Pro's commands to save the image to disk.

Once your scanner and software are installed, you select the scanner by choosing Select Source from Paint Shop Pro's File menu. A dialog box will display a list of the TWAIN sources available on your system. Select the desired source; you need do this only once during each session, and if there is only a single Twain source available, the step can be omitted altogether.

HIGHER PRICED SCANNERS

As you browse the scanner listings in a catalog, you may wonder why scanners with apparently similar capabilities—resolution and color depth—will differ widely in price. It's sort of like cars: You can have a 5-passenger, 18-miles-per gallon Hyundai, and you can also have a 5-passenger, 18-miles-per gallon Mercedes. More expensive scanners are likely to have higher-quality components, including lower noise CCDs, which give superior images. Higher price may also mean quieter mechanisms, faster scanning times, and a more advanced light source for improved color balance and repeatability.

With the source selected, next choose Acquire from the File menu. Your scanning program will be displayed on top of the Paint Shop Pro window. The details of the next steps will differ from one program to the next, but generally the following procedures are involved:

1. The scanner makes a preview scan of the entire original and displays it on screen.

2. The scanning program analyzes the image and makes certain automatic settings based on the nature of the image.

3. The user selects the region to be included in the final scan. If desired, changes to other settings (such as resolution or color depth) are made at this time.

4. The final scan is taken and the image is displayed in Paint Shop Pro.

The scanner settings that you need to be aware of are color depth and resolution. The quality of the final result depends on selecting the proper settings for the original you are scanning and for the intended destination. Proper scanner settings when scanning a color photograph to be printed will differ from the settings required when scanning a black-and-white photograph to be displayed on a Web page. We'll explore various settings in the following section.

Scanner Settings

I have been referring to scanner settings in terms of resolution and color depth, but with most scanning software you do not set these parameters directly. Instead, the software will permit you to select the type of original as well as the intended destination. For example, my scanner software lets

me choose Color Photograph as the type of original and Screen as the destination, and the appropriate color depth and resolution settings will automatically be made. Figure 3.1 shows an example of Hewlett-Packard's DeskScan software displaying a preview image. You can see that the original type is set to Color Photo and the destination, or *path*, is set to Screen. The software will scan the final image with resolution and color depth settings appropriate for this type of original and this destination.

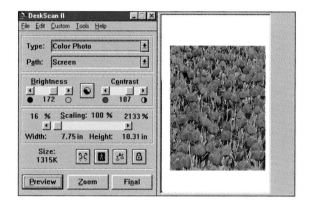

Figure 3.1 Scanner software lets you preview the image and specific scanner settings.

This method of setting scan parameters generally works perfectly well, and is also easy to use. Nevertheless, knowing more of the theory behind scanner settings will enable you to fine-tune the settings for optimum results and also to deal with scanning tasks not covered by the software's built-in settings.

Selecting Color Depth

One required scanner setting is color depth—the number of colors that will be captured in the final image. This setting is an easy one. For color photographs, you should always use the maximum number of colors available. Different scanner programs will have different terms for this setting, such as "millions of colors" or "high color" or "true color." This setting will permit the scanner to differentiate millions of different colors in the original image, necessary for accurate reproduction of color photographs.

There is another color-depth setting that you may use from time to time. This setting is typically called 256 Grays. With this setting, the scanner ignores colors and captures the image in black and white, or more precisely, in 256 levels of gray ranging from black to white. Use 256 Grays mode when scanning black-and-white photographs or when scanning a color image that you want to convert to black and white.

Selecting Scanner Resolution

Selecting the resolution of your scan is perhaps the most important choice you'll make. In selecting a resolution, you need to take into account the intended use of the scanned image. Here's why.

Just like the scan you make has a dots per inch resolution, what the image is displayed on does too. Whether the image is displayed on a screen or is printed on paper, there is a resolution associated with the output device. A computer monitor might have 72 dpi, while a color laser printer might be 600 dpi and an ink jet printer is typically 300 dpi. The optimum results are always obtained if the image's resolution matches the resolution of the output device. If they do not match, one of the following two results will occur:

- If the image resolution is lower than the output resolution, the display or printing process will interpolate the extra pixels that are needed and the final result will lose detail and sharpness.

- If the image resolution is higher than the output resolution, the display or printing process will discard the extra pixels. The result will look fine, but the image file will be unnecessarily large. You could have obtained the same quality result with lower resolution and a smaller file.

Determining The Ideal Resolution

Ideally, the resolution at which you scan will exactly match the intended output resolution. While display screens differ slightly, 72 or 90 dpi are the most common settings. Printers vary more, with values of 150 or 300 dpi normal in common ink jet printers. Some newer models offer higher resolution, however, so you need to check your printer's settings.

The ideal resolution setting for scanning also depends on the relative sizes of the original and the reproduction. If you plan to reproduce the image at the same size as the original, no adjustments are necessary—simply scan at the resolution of the output device. If, however, you will be printing or displaying the image at a different size, either larger or smaller than the original, you may need to make some adjustments when scanning.

Let's look at an example. Suppose you are scanning a 4×5 inch snapshot with the intention of printing it at 8×10 inch size on an ink jet printer with a 150 dpi resolution. If you scan at 150 dpi resolution, the scanned image will have 600 pixels vertically (4 inches times 150 dpi) and 750 pixels horizontally (5 inches times 150 dpi). When you enlarge the image to the final print size of 8×10 inches, the effective resolution will be only 75 dpi—the 750 horizontal pixels will be spread out over 10 inches (750 divided by 10 equals 75), and the same is true in the vertical dimension. Thus, for the best final printed output, you would need to scan the image at 300 dpi, which, in the final enlarged image, would give you a resolution that matches the printer.

A similar adjustment needs to be made if the output size is smaller than the original. Suppose you are scanning a 4×5 inch photo that is to be displayed on your Web page at half size, 2×2-$\frac{1}{2}$ inches. If you scan at the 72 dpi typical of a computer display, the scanned image will be 288×360 pixels, which, when reduced to half size, will give a resolution of 144 dpi. This is twice as high as needed; you could scan at 36 dpi with no loss of final quality.

Puzzled? I can't say I blame you. Fortunately, there's a simple formula you can use to determine the ideal scanning resolution. First, let's define some terms:

- SR = ideal scanning resolution

- DR = resolution of final display device

- OW = width of the original being scanned

- DW = width at which the image will be printed or displayed

Then:

$$SR = DR \times DW / OW$$

With this formula, you can easily determine the ideal resolution at which you should scan.

Determining The Real-World Resolution

Unfortunately, things usually aren't that simple. There are a number of factors that can, and usually do, prevent you from using that "ideal" resolution when scanning:

- You are not sure of the final use of the image—how it will be reproduced and at what size.

Figure 3.2 A section of an image scanned at 75 dpi (top), 150 dpi (center), and 300 dpi (bottom).

- There are multiple uses intended for the image—for example, you want to make printed copies as well as display it on a Web page.

- The calculated ideal resolution is an intermediate value— such as 117 dpi—that is not supported by your scanner.

In these and other cases, the general rule is to "move up." In other words, you should always move to a higher resolution rather than to a lower one. Thus, if you cannot use the "ideal" resolution of, say, 117 dpi, you should scan at 150 dpi rather than at 100 dpi. Likewise, if you plan to use the image for printing at 300 dpi as well as for screen display at 72 dpi, use 300 dpi when scanning if possible.

Figure 3.2 provides a visual indication of the image quality differences that different scanning resolutions give. I scanned a photograph at 75 dpi, 150 dpi, and 300 dpi and then cropped the same half-inch wide section from the image. When they are printed at the same size, the resolution differences are quite obvious.

Scanning at a higher resolution captures the maximum amount of information, or detail, from the original. You can always throw away some of that information by reducing the image's resolution after scanning, but you cannot regain information if the image was scanned at too low a resolution. The process of changing an image's resolution is called *resampling*. (Resampling is covered in Chapter 7.) If, for example, you scanned an image at 300 dpi for printing, you could resample it at 72 dpi for screen display.

What if you have no idea what the image will be used for? The rule of thumb then is to scan it at the highest possible resolution, resampling it if needed later on. There's a problem, however, in that high-resolution images will fill up your hard drive quickly. Table 3.1 lists the file sizes that result from scanning a 4×5 inch original in 8 bits per color mode at each of several resolution settings.

Table 3.1 File sizes for a 4×5 image scanned at different resolutions in true color mode.

Resolution	File size
72 dpi	0.3MB
150 dpi	1.35MB
200 dpi	2.4MB
300 dpi	5.4MB
600 dpi	21.6MB

I don't know about you, but my hard drive does not have room for too many 21MB files. Clearly there is a tradeoff to be made when selecting the resolution for scanning images. For color photographs, I suggest you follow the following guidelines if you do not know how the final image will be used:

- 150 dpi is the minimum that gives acceptable results.

- 200 dpi is perhaps the best compromise, giving very good image quality without creating monster files.

- 300 dpi provides excellent image quality, but the files are more than twice as large as with 200 dpi.

Sharpening

Almost all scanning software offers a sharpening filter option. When this filter is enabled, the scanning software processes the image data to increase the sharpness of the image. Sharpening can significantly improve the final appearance of some images, as shown in Figure 3.3. The original image was scanned with the sharpening option turned off, then scanned again with sharpening enabled. There is an obvious improvement in the second image.

Figure 3.3 An image scanned without (left) and with (right) sharpening.

UNEVEN BRIGHTNESS?

If you are using a flatbed scanner and your
scanned images have uneven brightness—darker
on one edge— then try positioning the originals in
the center of the scanner's glass rather than the
scanner's edge. The lamps in some scanners,
particularly inexpensive ones, sometimes fall
off near the edges of the scanning area. Placing
the original in the center of the glass makes it
more difficult to scan the photo in straight, but
you'll get more even illumination.

There are two types of sharpening filters:

- A basic sharpening filter increases the apparent sharpness by increasing the overall contrast in the image.

- An unsharp masking filter increases apparent sharpness by selectively increasing contrast only along edges in the image. This type of sharpening was used in Figure 3.3.

Generally speaking, an unsharp mask filter provides better results than a basic sharpening filter. The question still remains, however, whether you should use sharpening at all. Your scanner software's automatic setting may give perfectly good results, but if you want to control sharpening yourself here, are some things to consider:

- Sharpening tends to be more desirable with images that will be printed, and less important for images that will be displayed on screen.

- Images with a lot of detail, such as distant landscapes or city scenes, tend to react well to sharpening. Images with significant areas of low detail, such as photographs of faces, are more likely to react poorly to sharpening.

- Higher-resolution images are more amenable to sharpening than are low resolution images.

If you are unsure about a specific image, you can always scan it both with and without sharpening and see which one you prefer. Remember that you can apply sharpening later in Paint Shop Pro. If you are not sure, perhaps the best approach is to scan your images without sharpening and then sharpen them later in Paint Shop Pro if needed. Paint Shop Pro offers both the basic sharpening filter and the unsharp mask filter.

WHAT IS CONTRAST?

The term *contrast* refers to the differences between the light and dark areas of an image. A photo taken in sunlight, for example, will have higher contrast than one taken on a foggy day.

Summing Up

A scanner is an important tool for most people working in digital photography. You'll find a scanner particularly useful if, like many people, you have a drawer full of old family and vacation pictures. Modern scanners and scanning software make basic scanning an almost automatic process. With the information you learned in this chapter, you are ready to go beyond the basics to have complete control over your scans.

PART 2

MAKING IMPROVE- MENTS

TOO LIGHT,
TOO 4 DARK

The brightness of a photograph is an important part of the image's overall appearance. The darkest possible elements in a photo are pure black, and the brightest are pure white. In between these extremes are seemingly countless levels of brightness. A photograph's overall brightness is controlled by the exposure when it is taken. The relative brightness of the photo's individual parts depends more on the nature of the subject. For instance, a shiny car bumper will, of course, be brighter than the black tires.

Despite the generally excellent accuracy of automatic exposure systems, photographs sometimes receive too much or too little exposure, resulting in an image that is too bright or too dark, overall. Likewise, the nature of your subject matter may result in areas of the photograph being too bright or too dark. For example, a patch of sunlight in an otherwise shaded area may distract the viewer from the main subject of the photograph. Fortunately, digital image manipulation provides the means to correct many brightness problems. In this chapter, you will learn how this is done.

Brightness In Digital Images

Each pixel in a digital image has a *brightness* associated with it; a pixel's brightness is also referred to as its *luminance*. A pixel's luminance is expressed as a number ranging from 0 to 255. In a monochrome (black-and-white) image, a pixel's luminance is the same as the pixel value, which also ranges from 0 to 255 representing the gray scale from black to white. In a color image, where a pixel is represented by its red, green, and blue values (referred to as its RGB value) each ranging from 0 to 255, the luminance is the average of the red, green, and blue values. Thus, brightness is independent of color. Different colors can have the same luminance and their subjective brightness will be identical—that is, they will appear equally bright to the viewer. Thus, a red area of the image can appear equally bright as a blue area if the luminances are the same. For example, a red area comprised of pixels with RGB values 200,0,0 will have the same brightness as a blue area with RGB value 0,0,200—each color has the same luminance value of 200. This is illustrated in Figure 4.1.

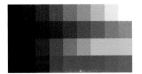

Figure 4.1 Different colors with the same luminance value appear equally bright.

The color blocks in each of the image's columns have the same luminance, starting at 0 in the far left column and moving in equal increments to 255 in the far right column. Within each column, the red, green, and blue blocks, as well as the gray block, appear equally bright.

Paint Shop Pro lets you modify an image's brightness (we'll see how later in the chapter) by increasing or decreasing the pixels' luminance values while still maintaining the relative color balance.

Image Contrast

Closely related to brightness is the *contrast* of an image. An image's contrast refers to its luminance range. The wider the range, the greater the difference between the brightest and darkest areas, and the higher the contrast. There is no "proper" level

CONTRASTING EDGES

When you examine Figure 4.1 closely, you should notice that the left edge of each color block appears brighter than the right edge. Why is this? Within each block, all pixel values are identical (which you can verify by loading the image into Paint Shop Pro and using the Eyedropper tool to display RGB values for individual pixels). This apparent distortion is a perceptual phenomenon caused by your visual system. The left edge of each color block looks brighter because it is next to a darker region—the block to the immediate left. Likewise, the right edge of each block appears darker because it is adjacent to a brighter area.

To use the Eyedropper tool, you must first display the Color Palette by selecting Color Palette from the View menu. Click on the Eyedropper button on the toolbar, and then point at any area of the image. The Color Palette displays the pixel's RGB value from which you can calculate the luminance.

of contrast because different subjects have inherently different contrasts. Figures 4.2 and 4.3 illustrate this. One photograph is high contrast and the other is low contrast, but each "works" because it accurately reproduces the appearance of the original subject.

Figure 4.2 This Greek wall relief is naturally low contrast and would not benefit from increased contrast.

The definition of contrast that I gave earlier is technically accurate, but it can be misleading. If an image's contrast is simply considered to be the difference between the brightest pixel and the darkest pixel, then any image with areas of pure black and pure white, no matter how small the areas, would have maximum contrast. Look again at Figure 4.2. If you search hard enough, you will find a few areas of pure black as well as a few areas of pure white. Thus, by the technical definition, this photo has the same contrast as Figure 4.3. This is obviously not the case, because one photo is clearly high contrast in appearance and the other is low contrast, and after all, it is the visual appearance of photographs we are interested in.

The difference in the visual contrast between these images is due to two factors. First is the juxtaposition of bright and dark areas. In Figure 4.3, there are many edges where a bright area is adjacent to a dark area. These edges produce a high contrast

Figure 4.3 The wrought iron design on this Paris doorway is a high contrast subject and would not be nearly as attractive if the contrast were lower.

appearance. Figure 4.2 differs in that brightness changes happen gradually—almost every region of the image is adjacent to a region with closely similar luminance values. There are few, if any, bright/dark edges in this figure.

The second factor is the distribution of pixel luminance values. In Paint Shop Pro, you can view a graph of an image's luminance values by selecting Histogram Window from the View menu. In the Histogram window, be sure that only the Luminance box is checked (you'll learn about the red, green, and blue histograms in Chapter 5). Figure 4.4 shows the luminance histogram for the image in Figure 4.2.

Here's how to read a luminance histogram: The horizontal axis represents luminance values from 0 at the left to 255 at the right. The vertical axis represents the number of pixels. The graph line shows how many pixels in the image have each luminance level. You can see from the histogram in Figure 4.4 that the corresponding image (Figure 4.2) has very few pixels with low luminance, in the range of 0 to about 100. It also has few pixels at the high end of the luminance scale, above 240 (approximately). The majority of the image's pixels are bunched together in the high/middle luminance range, values approximately between 110 and 240, resulting in a low contrast image.

Compare this with the histogram of the image in Figure 4.3 (see Figure 4.5). Most of the image's pixels are either at the low end or the high end of the luminance scale, with relatively few pixels at the intermediate luminance levels. Such spreading out of luminance values is associated with a high contrast appearance.

Changing Contrast

When you use Paint Shop Pro's tools to change an image's contrast, what exactly happens? Increasing the contrast causes dark areas to become darker and light areas to become lighter. Conversely, decreasing the contrast causes dark areas to become lighter and light areas to become darker. Figures 4.6 through 4.8 illustrate this effect. Figure 4.6 contains 16 shades of gray ranging from black on the left to near white on the right.

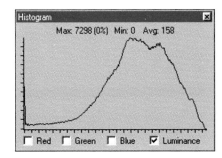

Figure 4.4 The luminance histogram for the image in Figure 4.2 reveals a low contrast luminance distribution.

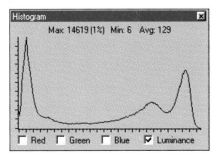

Figure 4.5 The luminance histogram for the image in Figure 4.3 reveals a high contrast luminance distribution.

Figure 4.6 The original image spans pure black to near white in 16 steps.

Figure 4.7 The image in Figure 4.6 with increased contrast.

Figure 4.8 The image in Figure 4.6 with decreased contrast.

The result of increasing the contrast is shown in Figure 4.7. You can see that several of the steps that were dark gray are now black, several steps that were light gray are now white, and the separation between the steps in the middle is increased.

Figure 4.8 shows the original image with reduced contrast. The black is changed to dark gray, the white is changed to light gray, and the separation between the steps is decreased.

Changes to an image's contrast can have a major impact on its appearance. We'll see just how major later in the chapter.

Candle Power
Changing an image's overall brightness

Figure 4.9 shows a photograph that I took in Notre Dame cathedral in Paris. As the photo makes evident, it was quite dark in the building. Even though I had a flash, I did not want to use it for two reasons. First, the flash would have destroyed the delicate and beautiful light cast by the candles. Second, I did not want to disturb other people in the church. I knew the light level was too low for a technically "good" exposure, but I thought it was worth a try. I braced my camera and took a few shots. Due to the slow shutter speed most, of them were too blurry. The one shown here, however, had promise. The only problem is that it is too dark.

Here are the steps required to brighten the photograph:

1. Use the File|Open command to load the original image into Paint Shop Pro.

2. Select Adjust from the Colors menu, then select Brightness/ Contrast. The Brightness/Contrast dialog box will be displayed (see Figure 4.10). Instead of using the menus, you can press Shift+B to display this dialog box.

3. In the % Brightness box, enter the value by which you want to change the image's brightness to. Positive values

Figure 4.9 The original photograph is too dark.

Figure 4.10 You use the Brightness/ Contrast dialog box to change image brightness.

SAVE COPIES

When manipulating image brightness, it is always a good idea to keep the original image and save the modified image under a new name. You might think that you could get the original just by reversing the change—for example, increasing the brightness of an image whose brightness was previously decreased. This is not always true, and "reversing" your brightness changes often will not give a result that is identical to the original image. For this reason, I advise you to always keep a copy of the original unmodified image in case you want to return to it. This is a good idea for any image manipulation, not just brightness changes.

increase the brightness while negative values decrease it. You can also click the Up or Down arrow next to the box to change the value.

4. As you change the % Brightness value, the thumbnail image in the dialog box shows the effects of the change. Click on the Preview button to temporarily apply the change to the original full-size image. (I recommend using Preview to evaluate the changes, as I find the thumbnail image too small for accurate evaluation.)

5. When you have found the desired setting, click on OK to permanently apply the change to the image. (I used a setting of +16.)

6. Use the File|Save As command to save the modified image under a different name.

Figure 4.11 shows the final result. Through the magic of digital photography, we have shed some extra light on a scene that happened thousands of miles away and years ago.

Figure 4.11 After being brightened, the image is much more attractive.

NO TRIPOD?

You may sometimes find yourself in a low-light situation that will force a slow shutter speed, but you either do not have or do not want to use a tripod. You can greatly improve your chances of a successful photo by simply bracing yourself against a solid object, such as a tree or door frame.

Limitations Of Brightness Changes

The ability to increase or decrease the brightness of a digital photograph is indeed a powerful tool, but there are limitations. The most evident limitation is that brightness change cannot add detail lacking in the original photograph. If an area of the photograph is solid black, increasing the brightness can make that area gray instead of black, but it cannot supply the details that were present in the original scene. For example, a dark, shadowed area in a sunlit scene may contain details that were obvious to the eye at the time the photo was taken, but if this region is recorded as solid black by the camera, then there is no way to retrieve those details. The same is true for areas of an image that are pure white—decreasing the brightness can change them to light gray, but cannot retrieve detail.

Row Your Boat
Changing the brightness of part of an image

I love boats, and as a result I have lots of photographs of boats. Not all of them turn out exactly like I plan, however. The photo shown in Figure 4.12 is an example of this. I like the quiet colors and the composition of the image, but there's one problem that you have probably already spotted: the sunlit concrete dock in the foreground is too bright. Can this be fixed? You bet.

We could reduce the brightness of the dock by darkening the entire photo, but that won't work because the rest of the image—the boat and the lake—are just about right. The rectangular Selection tool is not much help because the area we need to darken is not a rectangle. The Freehand tool is a possibility, but do you really want to try to draw an accurate line around the edges of the dock? Neither do I.

We will use Paint Shop Pro's Magic Wand tool, which allows you to select an irregularly shaped area based on similarity of color or brightness. Here's how it works: You click on a spot within the area that you want to select; this will serve as the seed pixel. The Magic Wand tool "looks" at pixels adjacent to the seed pixel and determines if they are sufficiently similar to it. If so, they are included in the selection; if not, the selection boundary has been reached. This process continues in all directions from the seed pixel until a closed selection has been defined.

When using the Magic Wand, you specify how "similarity" is defined, either in terms of RGB value or brightness. (There's a third similarity setting, Hue, but we won't be using it in this book.) You also specify how close a match is required, and how sharp the selection edges will be. This will all make more sense when you see it in action. Let's get to work.

Figure 4.12 The bright white foreground in this photograph detracts from the main subject.

Figure 4.13 Setting the Magic Wand's parameters.

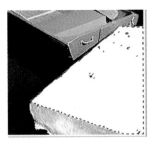

Figure 4.14 The area selected by the Magic Wand tool is outlined with a dashed line.

Selecting An Irregular Area

The first step in improving the rowboat photograph is to create a selection that includes only the bright area of the dock.

1. Load the original image into Paint Shop Pro.

2. Select the Magic Wand tool. The Magic Wand settings will be displayed on the toolbar (Figure 4.13).

3. Set the parameters as shown here (you may want to experiment with different settings to see how they work):

   • **Match Mode: Brightness**. Adjacent pixels will be selected or rejected based on their luminance.

   • **Tolerance: 20**. Adjacent pixels will be included in the selection if their luminance is within 20, plus or minus, of the seed pixel's luminance.

   • **Feather: 0**. The edges of the selection will be sharp.

4. Click in the area you want selected. Paint Shop Pro will calculate the selection and display an animated dashed line on its border, as shown in Figure 4.14.

If the selected area is not what you want, press Shift+N to remove the selection. Then change the Magic Wand settings and try again.

Darkening The Selected Area

Once you have the desired area selected, changing its brightness is a simple matter. In fact, it's no different from changing the brightness of an entire image, as you did in Project 1. That's how Paint Shop Pro works—manipulations apply to the selected area of the image; if no area is selected, they apply to the entire image. Here are the required steps:

1. Press Shift+B to display the Brightness/Contrast dialog box (shown earlier in Figure 4.10).

2. Be sure that the % Contrast box contains 0, since we do not want to change the image contrast in this project.

3. Enter the desired brightness change in the % Brightness box. (I used -20, but you may prefer a slightly different value.)

4. Click on Preview to see what the change looks like when applied to the original image. Click on OK to make the change permanent.

5. Save the modified image under a new name.

Figure 4.15 shows the final result. Without the glaring white dock in the foreground, the image is much more cohesive and peaceful.

Some readers may be thinking that the change we made to the photo is rather subtle. Is it really worth the effort to make changes like this one? Who is going to notice? First of all, and perhaps most important, *you* will notice. Taking pride in your work and always striving for the best possible result is the only way to approach digital imaging, at least in my opinion. And it's likely that other people will notice, too. It might just be your neighbors thinking that you have the best family album in town, but it might also be a client giving you that coveted assignment because your images just edged out the competition. Don't settle for "good enough."

Figure 4.15 With the brightness of the dock reduced, the image is much improved.

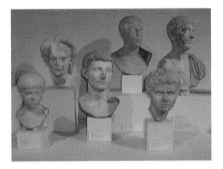

Figure 4.16 The contrast is too low in the original photograph.

PROJECT 3

It's A Bust!
Changing image contrast

The photograph in Figure 4.16 was taken in the Metropolitan Museum of Art in New York City. It shows some ancient busts that were on display, and while I have forgotten whether they are Greek or Roman, I do like the image. Unfortunately, it is rather "flat" and lacking in contrast, having been taken under the museum's unflattering fluorescent lights. I could not use a flash because of museum rules. Even if I could have used a flash, it probably would not have worked because of the glass case between me and the figures. With digital manipulation, this image can be saved. Here are the steps required.

1. Use the File|Open command to load the image into Paint Shop Pro.

2. Select Colors|Adjust|Brightness/Contrast, or press Shift+B, to display the Brightness/Contrast dialog box. (You saw this dialog box previously in Figure 4.10.) Be sure that the % Brightness box is set to 0 (it will "remember" your previous entry) as we do not need to change brightness in this project.

3. In the % Contrast box, enter the value by which you want to change the image's contrast. Positive values increase contrast and negative values decrease it.

4. As you change the % Contrast value, you can preview the change in the thumbnail image or, by clicking the Preview button, in the original full-size image.

5. When you have found the desired setting, click on OK to permanently apply the change to the image. (I used a setting of +25.)

6. Use the File|Save As command to save the modified image under a different name.

Figure 4.17 Increasing the contrast by 25 percent results in a significant improvement.

Figure 4.17 shows the end result. The moderate change in contrast makes a very noticeable difference, resulting in an image that is clearer and has more apparent detail.

Other Brightness And Contrast Adjustments

So far, we have covered the most important digital manipulations for dealing with image brightness and contrast. Paint Shop Pro offers a couple of additional tools, and while I won't be demonstrating them in a project, you need to know about them so you can experiment on your own.

Gamma Adjustment

Gamma adjustment is related to the so-called *midtones* in an image—the parts of the image that are neither very dark nor very bright. In a majority of photos, the midtones make up most of the image and are therefore very important in the image's overall quality. The importance of midtones is related to the fact that we tend to perceive brightness relative to the surroundings. Thus, an object will appear brighter when viewed against a dark background than when viewed against a light background. This is illustrated in Figure 4.18. The two red patches have identical RGB values, but the one with the dark background is perceived as being brighter than the one with the light background.

Paint Shop Pro's Gamma adjustment allows you to modify the midtones in an image without affecting the high and low values. Gamma is expressed as a numerical value. A Gamma of 1 is "normal," or the same as the original image. Gamma values less than 1 darken the midtones, while Gamma values greater than 1 lighten the midtones.

To change Gamma in Paint Shop Pro, select Adjust from the Colors menu, then select Gamma Correction, or press the shortcut key Shift+G. The Gamma Correction dialog box (Figure 4.19) lets you specify the Gamma value and preview the effects, much like the other adjustment dialog boxes you have used. I suggest that you spend some time experimenting with Gamma correction. Once you get a feel for what it can do, you will probably find it to be a useful tool.

TALKING ABOUT VALUES

The dark areas in an image are sometimes referred to as the low values or shadows, and the bright areas are called the high values or highlights.

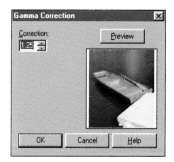

Figure 4.18 Identical red patches are perceived as having different brightness values because of their backgrounds.

Figure 4.19 The Gamma Correction dialog box lets you adjust an image's midtones.

Figure 4.20 The Highlight/Midtone/ Shadow dialog box is used to selectively adjust image brightness.

Highlight/Midtone/Shadow Adjustment

The Highlight/Midtone/Shadow adjustment provides another way for you to adjust brightness in your digital images. You can emphasize either the shadows or the highlights, and you can also selectively brighten or darken the midtones. To open the Highlight/Midtone/Shadow dialog box (Figure 4.20), press Shift+M, or select Colors|Adjust|Highlight/Midtone/Shadow.

This dialog box has three settings:

- **Highlight**. This setting can only be decreased from its normal value of 100. It adds luminance proportionally, with lighter pixels increased more and darker pixels increased less.

- **Midtone**. This setting can be increased or decreased from its normal value of 50. It either brightens or darkens the image's midtones without affecting the highlights or shadows.

- **Shadows**. This setting can only be increased from its normal value of 0. It removes luminance proportionally, with darker pixels decreased more and brighter pixels decreased less.

Summing Up

Brightness adjustments are some of the most important manipulations you have available for improving your digital photographs. Because it is so significant, graphics programs such as Paint Shop Pro provide a powerful array of tools for manipulating brightness. You may think that some of these tools perform similar actions, and you are not too far off base. There is indeed some overlap between the actions of, for example, Brightness/Contrast adjustment and Highlight/Midtone/ Shadow adjustment. They are not identical, however, and with some experience you will become comfortable with selecting the best tool for the job at hand.

CORRECTING
COLOR
BALANCE

5

Most of your digital photographs will be color. In fact, unless you scan some old black-and-white photos, almost all of your photographs will be color. Color is what people want, and whether it's for your Web page or your family album, you will probably be working with color images.

There's a downside to color, however—it is one more thing that can go wrong. Maybe the bright red roses in the photograph are not quite as red as they were in real life. Perhaps Uncle Joe's face came out a bit on the greenish side because you photographed him under fluorescent lights. Heck, maybe Uncle Joe really is green, but you still don't want him looking that way in the photo! Fortunately, digital photography gives you a great deal of freedom to manipulate the colors in your photos, either to correct errors or to provide that extra bit of creativity that will set your images apart from others. But before getting to this chapter's projects, you will need to know something about how computer color works and about the tools for working with color that Paint Shop Pro gives you.

The Primary Colors

Any color can be created by combining the three primary colors—red, green, and blue—in the proper proportions. And I do mean *any* color—from blacks and grays to pure white, from palest pink to scarlet, from mauve to chartreuse. Primary colors are a result of the way the human eye works, but that's something you don't really need to understand (and something I'm not about to explain!). In order to effectively manipulate the color in your photographs, however, you will need to know how the primary colors work.

In a color digital photo, each pixel's color is determined by the relative intensities of the three primaries, known as its RGB (red-green-blue) value. These are three numbers ranging from 0 to 255, one for each of the primary colors. Zero means the primary color is absent, while 255 means it is at its maximum intensity. An RGB value of 0,0,0 is black, 255,255,255 is white, 0,255,0 is

USE YOUR COMPUTER DISPLAY'S FULL POTENTIAL

When working with digital images, you should set your computer screen to display as many colors as possible. Right-click anywhere on your PC's desktop and select Properties from the pop-up menu to open the Display Properties dialog box. On the Settings tab, pull down the Color Palette list and select True Color (preferred) or High Color. You may sacrifice screen resolution to use these color modes, but it is next to impossible to do any serious photo work in 256 color mode.

bright green, and so on. Table 5.1 presents some other examples of RGB colors, and Figure 5.1 illustrates how the primary colors combine.

A color also has a *luminance*, which can be thought of as its brightness. Luminance is the average of the color's RGB values, and therefore also ranges from 0 to 255. The RGB values 255,255,255 give the highest luminance, which makes perfect sense because that color is pure white. Likewise, 0,0,0, or black, has the lowest luminance. Different colors can have the same luminance. For example, RGB 0,128,255 is a medium blue and RGB 255,0,128 is reddish purple, but the luminance values are the same because their RGB values have the same average.

Colors In Paint Shop Pro

Paint Shop Pro provides several tools for working with color. You can determine the RGB value of any pixel in a photograph with the Eyedropper tool. With a photo open in Paint Shop Pro, select the Eyedropper tool, then point at the area on the photograph in which you're interested (you don't have to click). On the right side of the screen, the Current Color panel of the Color Palette (Figure 5.2) will display the RGB values of the pixel you are pointing to, as well as a swatch of that color. If the Color Palette is not visible, select Color Palette from the View menu to display it.

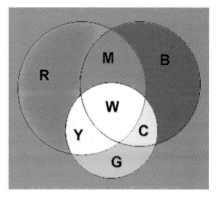

Figure 5.1 When two additive primaries combine, they produce one of the subtractive primaries (cyan, magenta, yellow). When all three additive primaries combine, they produce white.

Figure 5.2 The Current Color panel displays the RGB value and a swatch of the pixel color that you point to with the Eyedropper tool.

ENLARGE YOUR VIEW

Before using the Eyedropper tool, you may want to magnify the image so you can more easily pick out specific pixels. Click the Zoom icon, then click one or more times on the image until the image size is what you want. To return to normal view, press Ctrl+- (the minus key on the numeric keypad) one or more times until the image returns to the original size.

Table 5.1 Some examples of RGB values and their resulting colors.

RGB Values	Color
255,0,0	Bright red
240,0,125	Reddish purple
128,128,128	Middle gray
127,246,116	Pale green
180,190,3	Muddy yellow

PUZZLED ABOUT PRIMARIES?

Some readers may be thinking that I've got the primary colors wrong—aren't red, blue, and yellow the primary colors? Yes, but those are the *subtractive* primaries, while red, green, and blue are the *additive* primaries. The subtractive primaries come into play when you are mixing paints, with the resulting color being a product of the colors the paint absorbs. Remember that white light, from the sun or a lamp, contains all colors in roughly equal proportions. When white light illuminates a blue object, it looks blue because all of the colors of the light except blue are absorbed, or subtracted, and only the blue light is reflected back to your eyes. Likewise, when you mix blue and yellow paint the resulting mixture absorbs all colors except green and hence appears green to us.

Technically, the subtractive "blue" primary is called cyan and the subtractive "red" primary is called magenta. The additive primaries are applicable when using light directly—when adding colors together. This is how a computer screen works. You can see this clearly if you take three flashlights and cover one with red cellophane, one with green cellophane, and one with blue cellophane. In a dark room, shine the red light on a white surface, then shine the green light so it partially overlaps the green. Where the red and green lights mix, you see yellow.

You can also use Paint Shop Pro's Histogram window to view an analysis of the photo's overall color and luminance distribution. With the photo active, select Histogram Window from the View menu. Figure 5.3 shows a photo of Times Square in New York City, and Figure 5.4 shows the photo's histogram.

How do you interpret the information in the histogram? The horizontal axis of the histogram represents the values 0 to 255, the same range that RGB color values and luminance values can take. On the histogram, there are four lines, one for each of the primary colors and a fourth for luminance (you can select which lines are displayed using the checkboxes under the histogram). The height of each line represents the proportion of pixels with corresponding values for that color component. For example, if a photo has a lot of pixels with blue values between 50 and 200, and relatively few pixels with blue values above or below that range, then the blue histogram line will be high in the middle and low at both ends. Similarly, if a photo has a lot of bright reds and a lot of dark reds, but few middle reds, the red line in the histogram will be high at both ends and low in the middle.

Let's look at Figure 5.4 and relate the histogram curves to the original photo. I've listed the main features here:

- The red, green, and blue peaks at the right side of the histogram represent the color values in the sky. The sky is a fairly uniform bluish-gray, so this is what you would expect—similar contributions of the three primary colors with blue having a slight predominance (as indicated by the blue peak being farther to the right, indicating higher blue values).

- The Luminance peak, which coincidentally overlaps the green curve, represents the luminance of the pixels in the sky.

Figure 5.3   The Histogram window can help you analyze the overall colors in a photograph, such as this one of New York's Times Square.

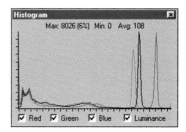

Figure 5.4   The histogram of the photograph in Figure 5.3.

TRUST YOUR EYES

If your eyes tell you a photograph looks okay, then don't worry about the histogram, even if you think the curves are "wrong" in some way. When your eyes tell you something is off in a photo's colors, then the Histogram can be a useful tool for identifying and fixing the problem.

- The gentle "hill" near the middle of the histogram corresponds to the pixels in the four signs on the building. The red component is strongest, as you would expect, due to the two red neon signs.

- The double-peaked hill at the left end of the histogram shows the pixels from the dark areas of the buildings.

The Histogram can be a useful tool, but it takes a bit of getting used to before you can mentally relate histogram curves to colors in a specific photograph. There's no substitute for practice, so I suggest that you examine the histograms of your photos on a regular basis.

SELECTION HISTOGRAMS

The Histogram window always displays the histogram of the entire photograph. At times, however, you may want to view a histogram of the colors in a portion of the photograph. You can do so indirectly, as follows:

1. Select the region of interest using either the Selection, Freehand, or Magic Wand tool.

2. Press Ctrl+C to copy the selection to the clipboard.

3. Press Ctrl+V to paste the selection as a new image.

4. View the histogram of the new image, which will be the same as the originally selected area.

The Central Park Blues
Cropping, adjusting brightness, and fixing color

Figure 5.5 shows a picture I took near Central Park in New York City of one of the horse-drawn carriages that are extremely popular with tourists. While I really like the subject of the photo, one problem was immediately obvious as soon as I saw it on my screen: The photo is too blue. The entire photo has an overall bluish cast that is very unpleasant. There are some other problems, too: The photo could benefit from cropping so the main subject is larger, and it might benefit from some brightening (increased luminance) as well. But clearly, the color balance is the main problem. Let's set about cropping first, then adjust the brightness, and leave the most serious problem—the bluish cast—for last.

Cropping The Photograph

In deciding how to crop the photograph, there were two main things I noticed:

- The lamp post, the car, and the pedestrians on the left side of the photo are distracting.

- There is too much empty sidewalk in the foreground.

Therefore, we want to crop the photograph to remove these areas. In the final image, the horse, driver, and carriage will fill most of the space. Here are the steps to follow:

Figure 5.5 The original photograph of a horse-drawn carriage in Central Park.

1. Use the File, Open command to load the original image into Paint Shop Pro.

2. Click on the Selection tool.

3. Using the mouse, point to the top-left corner of the area to be cropped. I used the coordinates 100, 12. Remember, you can see the current coordinates in the status bar.

4. Hold down the mouse button and drag the cursor to the lower-right corner of the crop area (the coordinates I used were 510, 335). Release the mouse button. Your screen will look like Figure 5.6.

Figure 5.6   Selecting the area to be cropped.

5. Copy the selected area to the clipboard. There are three ways to do this: Press Ctrl+C, select Copy from the Edit menu, or click the Copy icon on the toolbar.

6. Close the original image by clicking the X in the upper-right corner of the title bar. Because you have not changed it, there is no need to save the image at this point because it already exists on disk.

7. Press Ctrl+V to paste the copied area into a new image. Your screen will now display an image consisting only of the cropped area.

8. Select Save from the File menu and assign a name to the new image.

Adjusting The Image Brightness

Our next task is to make the image brighter.

1. Press Shift+B or select Colors|Adjust|Brightness/Contrast to open the Brightness/Contrast dialog box. Drag the dialog box so it does not hide any of your image.

2. Use the % Brightness box to specify the change you want (I used 20). You can enter a number directly or click the up or down arrow to increase or decrease the value displayed. Positive values increase the image brightness while negative values decrease it.

3. As you make changes, the thumbnail image in the dialog box shows the effects of the change. Click the Preview button to temporarily apply the change to the main image so you can evaluate how it looks. Figure 5.7 shows a preview of the photo with its brightness increased 20 percent.

Figure 5.7   Previewing the effect of a 20 percent brightness increase.

4. Once you have found the proper brightness setting, click on OK in the dialog box to make the change permanent and close the dialog box. You could also click the Cancel button to revert to the original image.

Correcting The Color Balance

The final step in improving this image is to correct the color balance.

1. Press Shift+U or select Colors|Adjust|Red/Green/Blue to open the Red/Green/Blue dialog box (shown in Figure 5.8). It works similarly to the Brightness/Contrast dialog box that you just finished using.

Figure 5.8   Making the color balance correction.

COLOR BALANCE AND BRIGHTNESS

The brightness of a pixel can be expressed as the sum of its red, green, and blue values. If you increase the level of one or two colors, you will not only change the photo's color balance, but will also increase its overall brightness. Likewise, decreasing the level of one or two colors will darken the picture. Suppose, for example, that you have a photo that is too blue. Reducing the blue level by 15 may fix the color problem, but it will also darken the picture slightly. Increasing the red and green each by 15 will have the same effect on the color balance, because the relative contribution of blue will be 15 units less. The difference is that the picture will be brightened instead of darkened. Suppose, however, that the brightness is just right—what do you do then? Reduce the blue by 10, and increase the red and green each by 5. Blue is reduced by 15 units relative to red and green, but the overall brightness—the sum of red, green, and blue—remains unchanged. Table 5.2 provides some guidelines on how to handle color/brightness corrections.

Figure 5.9 The final image is superior to the original.

2. Enter values in the % Red, % Green, or % Blue boxes to increase (positive values) or decrease (negative values) the level of the corresponding color in the image. You can see the effects of your changes in the thumbnail image or in the main image by clicking on Preview. Experiment until you get the effect you want. I used -8 blue, +5 green, and +10 red (see the sidebar in this chapter *Color Balance And Brightness* for more details).

3. Don't forget to save the final image.

Our image is "Central Park Blues"—no more. The final result is shown in Figure 5.9. Compare this image with the original in Figure 5.5 and I think you'll agree that it is much better.

Table 5.2 Combining color and brightness corrections.

If the color is...	and the brightness is...		
	OK	**Too Dark**	**Too Light**
Too red	Decrease R, increase G and B by half as much	Increase G and B	Decrease R
Too green	Decrease G, increase R and B by half as much	Increase R and B	Decrease G
Too blue	Decrease B, increase R and G by half as much	Increase R and G	Decrease B
Too yellow	Decrease R and G, increase B by twice as much	Increase B	Decrease R and G

More Red, Please
Adjusting color

PROJECT 5

While some photographs benefit from an overall change in color balance, others require a more selective touch. The color may be fine in part of a photo, but may require adjustment in other parts. Figure 5.10 is a good example. Taken in London (where else?), this is a well-composed and appealing picture of a young palace guard. On examination, however, one major fault becomes apparent: the guard's red coat appears somewhat muted, not at all the vibrant scarlet that I remembered. For the photograph to have maximum impact, the red in the coat needs to be intensified.

The Paint Shop Pro tool that will permit us to make these changes is called the Magic Wand. Rather than requiring you to draw the boundaries of the area you would like to select, the Magic Wand automatically creates a selection of pixels similar in RGB value to the spot that you click. For example, if you have a picture of a yellow banana on a red table, you can click the banana and the Magic Wand tool will create a selection whose boundaries follow exactly the edges of the banana. This tool is extremely useful because such irregularly shaped selections are next to impossible to outline by hand. The Magic Wand tool has three settings that control how it operates:

Figure 5.10 This London palace guard's coat needs to be redder.

- The Match Mode determines how "similar" is defined. The two settings that are of interest to use are RGB, with which the final selection will include pixels whose RGB values are close to the selected pixel, and Brightness, with which the pixels' brightness (luminance) is used to determine similarity.

- The Tolerance setting determines how close a match to the original pixel's values is required. A Tolerance of 0 means that a pixel's RGB or luminance value must match exactly to be included in the selection, while a Tolerance of 30 would permit a match if the pixel's values are within 30 units.

MAGIC WAND SELECTIONS

The Magic Wand will select only similar pixels that are adjacent to the starting point. To select two or more separate areas, hold down the Shift key while clicking.

Figure 5.11 Using the style bar to set Magic Wand options.

- The Feather setting controls the sharpness of the selection's edges. You can set Feather between 0 (sharpest edges) and 20 (softest edges). Any changes you make in a feathered selection are blurred over the feathered region (this is difficult to explain but easy to see if you experiment).

To set the Magic Wand's options, you must display the style bar by selecting Style Bar from the View menu. The style bar displays the option settings for whatever tool is currently selected. Figure 5.11 shows the Magic Wand options on the style bar.

Selecting The Coat Areas

Here's how to select the red areas of the guard's coat.

1. Load the photo into Paint Shop Pro, and select the Magic Wand tool. If necessary, display the style bar by selecting View|Style Bar.

2. Set the Magic Wand's options to Match Mode: RGB, Tolerance: 10, Feather: 0. You'll probably have to experiment with the Tolerance setting to get the selection you want.

3. Click anywhere in the left area of the guard's coat. You'll see an animated, dashed line surrounding the selected area. Evaluate the selection to see whether it extends to the edges of the red area. With Tolerance set to 10, the selected area will be too small.

4. Press Shift+N to cancel the selection. Increase the Tolerance setting and try again. Repeat until you have found the Tolerance setting that accurately selects the entire area. (I found a Tolerance setting of 55 works well.)

5. Once you have selected the left area of the coat, hold down Shift and click on both the central and right areas of the guard's coat. You will now have three separate selections (each surrounded by an animated line) and are ready to adjust the color. Figure 5.12 shows the selected areas with their outlines.

Figure 5.12 The selected areas of the image are outlined by dashed lines.

Adjusting The Coat's Color

Now that you have selected the areas whose colors need adjustment, making the actual color changes is easy. In fact, it requires the same steps that you used in Project 4 to change the color of an entire photograph. That's how Paint Shop Pro works—color adjustments (and most other adjustments as well) are applied to any selected areas or, if there is no selection, to the entire image.

1. With the red areas of the coat selected as described in the previous paragraph, press Shift+U to display the Red/Green/Blue dialog box. You saw this dialog box in Figure 5.8.

2. Adjust the colors as desired, viewing the thumbnail preview in the dialog box or clicking the Preview button to temporarily apply the changes to the main image.

3. When you've got the color you want, click on OK to make the changes permanent. I liked a +35 red change, with no modifications to the green and blue levels.

4. Use the File|Save As command to save the modified image under a new name.

As you can see from Figure 5.13, the change is quite dramatic (compare with Figure 5.10). Now a proper "Redcoat," this young soldier looks well suited to guard the Queen.

Summing Up

The term "color photograph" suggests how important color is to the overall quality of a photo. I hope that this chapter's projects have brought that point home. The right colors can bring a photo to life, allowing it to convey to the viewer just the mood and message you intended. The wrong colors can turn an otherwise excellent image into something about as compelling as day-old oatmeal. In combination with the brightness adjustments discussed in Chapter 4, Paint Shop Pro's color manipulation tools provide the most frequently needed capabilities for transforming your digital photos into masterpieces.

ALWAYS SAVE THE ORIGINAL

No matter how bad you think the original image is, you never know when you might want to use it again. That's why you should always save modified images under a new name so the original file will remain unchanged on your disk.

Figure 5.13 The palace guard with a properly red coat.

RETOUCHING

6

Originally, the term *retouching* was used to refer to correcting physical faults in a photograph. A scratch in the negative or a crease in the print were corrected by retouching. The term has taken on a wider meaning, and it is sometimes used to refer to correcting flaws in the image itself. For example, if your model has a skin blemish, you can use some careful retouching to correct it. Skillful retouching can save photographs that were otherwise headed for the trash.

Before the digital age, retouching photographs was a time-consuming and demanding task. Retouchers worked with an impressive array of brushes, pencils, inks, paints, razor blades, and other tools. Now, digital technology has greatly simplified matters. Once an image is in digital form, you can accomplish in a few minutes what used to take hours (or could not be done at all). In this chapter, you'll learn how to improve your photographs by using digital retouching techniques. But before we get started, you'll need to learn something about the useful retouching tools available in Paint Shop Pro.

Tools For Retouching

Several of the graphics tools provided by Paint Shop Pro are particularly useful for retouching jobs. You'll learn how to use them in this section. Remember that the fundamentals of using Paint Shop Pro are covered in the Appendix.

Copy And Paste

One of the techniques you'll use most often for retouching your digital photographs is copy and paste. This is useful in photographs that have a blemished area similar or identical to an unblem-ished area. Simply copying a patch from the un-blemished area and pasting it over the blemished area is often all that's required to make the photo look as good as new. This technique is most valu-able when the blemish affects a relatively smooth area of the image, such as the sky. It can some-times be used successfully on patterned areas that have a repeating design, such as a brick wall.

The first step is to select the area to be copied. Paint Shop Pro offers two such tools to do this. The Selection tool lets you select geometrically shaped areas: rectangles, ellipses, circles, or squares. The Freehand tool lets you select an ir-regular area by drawing around it. (Details on using these tools can be found in the Appendix.) If you make an error in defining the area, press Shift+N to cancel the selection and start over. Remember, the selected area is surrounded by an animated dashed line.

Once you have selected the area to be copied, press Ctrl+C to copy it to the clipboard, then Ctrl+E to paste it into the image as a new selection. The pasted selection may or may not be visible depend-ing on its background, but you'll know where it is because the cursor will be positioned over it. Move the mouse and the selection moves with it. You do not need to hold down any buttons to perform this task.

Once you have the selection positioned where you want it, left-click to "drop" the selection onto the image. The selection will now have an animated line around it, and will no longer move with the mouse. It is still moveable, however, and is called a *floating* selection. At this point you have several actions open to you:

- To move the selection again, hold the cursor over it and drag it.

- To cancel the entire copy and paste operation, press Ctrl+Z or drag the floating selection completely outside the image area.

- To permanently paste the selection in its current location and remove the animated border, right-click on it.

- If you paste the selection and realize you made a mistake, you can press Ctrl+Z to return the selection to the floating state.

Painting Tools

Paint Shop Pro's painting tools are often useful for performing retouching tasks. The process of "painting" is similar in many ways to painting you learned how to do in art class. Paint Shop Pro allows you to specify the type, size, and shape of the brush, as well as the paint color and the texture of the "paper." Let's start by looking at how you select a paint color; then we'll get to the details of using the different brush types.

Selecting A Color

When you have an image open in Paint Shop Pro, there are two active colors. The *foreground* color is used for painting and drawing. The *background* color is what is "behind" the image, and is revealed if you erase part of an image. For retouching digital photographs, you will be most concerned with the foreground color. The Color Palette (Figure 6.1) is one way to select colors. If the Color Palette is not visible, select Color Palette from the View menu to display it.

The middle portion of the Color Palette is called the *Active Colors panel.* The Active Colors panel displays two overlapping rectangles in the current foreground and background colors. In Figure 6.1, for example, you can see that the foreground color is green and the background color is purple. Click on the two-headed arrow in the Active Colors panel to switch the foreground and background colors.

Figure 6.1 The Color Palette displays and can be used to change the foreground and background colors.

EVALUATING YOUR RETOUCHING EFFORTS

When determining if your retouching efforts have been successful—or whether a particular image needs retouching at all—it is important to evaluate the image as it is intended to be used. For example, an image that will be printed full-page should not be evaluated when it is displayed at a size of 2×3 inches on-screen—you may miss problems that will be obvious in the larger, printed version. Likewise, if an image is intended for thumbnail-size display on a Web page, there's no reason to evaluate it displayed full-screen.

You can change the active colors by pointing at the Select Color panel (in the upper part of the Color Palette). The cursor automatically changes to an eyedropper. When the eyedropper is over the desired color, left-click or right-click to make that color the foreground or background color, respectively. Note that changing the active colors has no immediate effect on the image and only alters the colors that are used for subsequent painting actions.

Selecting the active colors using the Color Palette is usually not the best approach when retouching a photograph. You want to select a color that accurately matches a color that already exists in the image. This is easily done by doing the following:

1. Activate the Eyedropper tool by clicking on the Dropper button on the toolbar.

2. Point to the desired color in the image.

3. Left- or right-click in the image to make that color the new foreground or background color, respectively.

The active colors can also be defined numerically, by specifying their red, green, and blue values. Here are the required steps:

1. Click on either the foreground or background color in the Active Colors panel, depending on which color you want to set. Paint Shop Pro displays the Color dialog box (Figure 6.2).

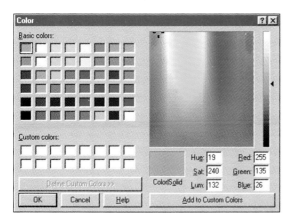

Figure 6.2 Use the Color dialog box to specify active colors with specific RGB value.

2. Enter the desired red, green, and blue values in the Red, Green, and Blue boxes.

3. Click on OK.

Paint Brushes

When you select the Paint Brushes tool by clicking on the corresponding toolbar button, you have access to an impressive array of painting tools. Paint Shop Pro's paint brush has several settings that control the appearance of the "paint" it applies to an image. These settings are displayed on the style bar when the Paint Brushes tool is active (Figure 6.3). If the style bar is not visible, select View|Style Bar to display it.

Figure 6.3   Using the style bar to set options for the Paint Brushes tool.

- **Brush type**. Determines whether the brush makes a mark like a pencil, a crayon, or another type of brush. You have six types from which to select.

- **Size**. Specifies the size of the brush, in pixels.

- **Shape**. Determines the shape of the applied color.

- **Paper texture**. Imitates various types of paper, controlling how the color is "absorbed" by the image.

Once you have selected brush options, simply point at the image and drag to apply color. Hold down the left mouse button to paint with the foreground color; hold down the right mouse button to paint with the background color. There is no way to explain the effects of these various brush set-

tings. You'll need to try them out yourself. The best way to do this is to create a blank image by selecting File|New and specifying White as the background color. Then you can practice painting with the various brushes and see what each does.

The Clone Brush

The Clone Brush tool is unlike Paint Shop Pro's regular paint brushes. Rather than painting with a color, the Clone Brush "paints" with a pixel pattern copied from another part of the image. To start, click in the image to identify the Clone Brush's source—the area you want copied. Then, paint in the same or another image. The source pixels are copied over the area where you are painting. Figure 6.4 shows the results of using the Clone Brush. The area "cloned" was the pink flowers in the lower-right corner of the image. The Clone Brush "painted" the pattern of the flowers and the surrounding area into the white area of the image.

The clone brush offers several options that control the way it operates. The Size, Shape, and Paper Texture options operate identically for the Clone Brush as they do for the regular brushes, as was explained previously. The other two Clone Brush options are:

- **Clone Mode**. This option determines what happens if you stop painting with the Clone Brush, then resume painting in another area without selecting a new source. With the Aligned option, the source moves accordingly, as if you had not stopped then resumed painting. With the Non-Aligned option, the source "resets" and acts as if you had just selected it.

Figure 6.4 The area on the left was painted with the Clone Brush, copying the pattern from the right part of the image.

RESTRICT YOUR PAINTING

To limit the area affected by painting, select the region first using any of Paint Shop Pro's selection tools. Painting will stop at the borders of the selection even if the brush moves outside the region.

- **Opacity**. This option determines how well the painted pixels cover what they are painted over. The permitted settings range from 128, where the coverage is complete, to 1, where the new pixels are almost completely transparent and the original background shows through strongly.

The Airbrush

The Airbrush tool is similar to the paint brush tools in many ways. Where it differs is that the color is "sprayed" on rather than being brushed on—similar to spray paint. This tool has four settings: Size, Shape, Opacity, and Paper Texture. These operate in the same manner as the options described earlier for the other tools. With the Airbrush, you can obtain soft edges that are difficult or impossible with the other brushes. For example, if you wanted to add a faint blush of pink to someone's cheek, the Airbrush tool would be the best choice.

The Retouch Tool

The Retouch tool, as its name implies, is designed to apply photo retouching effects to your images. Like the other tools discussed in this chapter, the Retouch tool has Size, Shape, Opacity, and Paper Texture options. It also offers six different retouching modes:

- **Lighten**. Increases brightness.

- **Darken**. Decreases brightness.

- **Soften**. Reduces contrast and smoothes edges.

- **Sharpen**. Increases contrast and emphasizes edges.

- **Emboss**. Causes foreground to appear raised from background by suppressing color and tracing edges in black.

- **Smudge**. Spreads colors, with an effect similar to smearing paint.

Note: Emboss and Smudge are not really useful for retouching, and will more likely be of use in creating special effects (as covered in later chapters).

Manipulating Individual Pixels

The most control you can have over an image is to manipulate individual pixels. At normal levels of magnification on your screen, the pixels of an image are not individually visible. With sufficient magnification, however, you can see and work with individual pixels. Figures 6.5 and 6.6 show an example. The area in Figure 6.5 marked by the white box is enlarged in Figure 6.6 by a factor of 8.

Figure 6.6 When enlarged by a factor of 8, you can see and manipulate individual pixels.

Figure 6.5 At normal magnification, the individual pixels are not apparent.

To magnify an image in Paint Shop Pro, select the Zoom tool, then click on the image one or more times until you reach the desired level of magnification. The spot you click on will remain centered. To reduce the magnification, right-click on the image. When the Zoom tool is active, you can also select a zoom ratio on the style bar. For example, 4:1 gives a magnification of 4 times normal, while 1:4 displays the image at one quarter normal size.

Once you have the desired level of magnification, select a color (as explained earlier in this chapter). Activate the Paint Brushes tool (or whichever tool is appropriate for the change you want to make) and set its width to 1 pixel. You can now click on individual pixels and change them. Zoom down to normal magnification to see how your changes will look, then zoom back up to continue working. Use the scroll bars in the image window to bring other parts of the image into view.

QUICK ZOOM

You can quickly zoom the active image by pressing Control and the plus sign (+) to increase the magnification or Control and the minus sign (-) to decrease the magnification. Note that you must use the + and − keys on the numeric keypad.

PROJECT 6

Major Repairs
Fixing tears, scratches, and other faults

Figure 6.7 shows a photograph of one of the old watch towers located along the rim of the Grand Canyon. It was taken with a regular film camera, and I made the mistake of leaving the print where my 3-year-old daughter could get hold of it. Before I could mount a rescue, she had torn off the top-right corner of the print. She also scribbled near the bottom of the photo with a crayon. There's a third fault, although I cannot blame my daughter for it: In the sky to the left of the tower you'll see a thin white line, which extends onto the tower itself. This was likely caused by a strand of a hair or scratch on the negative when the print was made. Clearly we have three different "repairs" to make before this image is usable. The final result, shown in Figure 6.8, shows how effective retouching can be when done properly.

Repairing The Tear

The tear will be relatively easy to fix because it is located in a region of the image that does not contain detail. We should be able to use a simple copy and paste to retouch this flaw. Note, however, that the sky is not completely uniform—it is dark

blue at the top and gradually gets lighter as you move down the photo. This means that the area that will be pasted over the tear must be copied from a region of the sky with the same brightness—in other words, near the top. Let's get started.

1. Load the original image into Paint Shop Pro.

2. Activate the Selection tool. Be sure its settings are Rectangular with Feather set to zero.

3. Select a region of sky at the top of the image, making it large enough to cover the entire torn area (Figure 6.8).

Figure 6.7   The original photograph is in desperate need of retouching.

Figure 6.8   Selecting the area of sky to be copied over the tear.

4. Press Ctrl+C to copy the selected area to the clipboard.

5. Press Ctrl+E to paste the selection into the image as a floating selection.

6. Move the selection until it is over the tear and completely covers it.

7. Left-click to "drop" the selection (Figure 6.9).

8. Press Shift+N to remove the border around the selection. The image now looks as if it had never been torn (Figure 6.10).

Getting Rid Of The Scratch

Retouching the scratch will be a little more difficult because it involves not only the sky area but also the tower, which has a lot of detail. The Clone Brush tool will provide better results than simply copying and pasting. Here are the steps to follow:

1. Press Control and the plus sign (+) one or more times (or use the Zoom tool) to enlarge the image sufficiently so the details of the scratch are clearly visible (Figure 6.11).

2. Activate the Clone Brush tool. Set its options to Clone mode: Non-Aligned; Size: 10; Shape: Round; Opacity: 128; Paper texture: none.

3. Right-click on a smooth area of the sky immediately adjacent to the scratch (Figure 6.12).

4. Point at the left end of the scratch and press and hold the left mouse button.

5. Drag over the scratch. Do not try to cover the scratch in one stroke. Rather, paint over a small part of the scratch, release the mouse button, and depress it again, then continue painting. If you don't like the results, you can undo the last stroke by pressing Ctrl+Z.

6. If the copy appears too dark or too light, select another color source by right-clicking on a different region of sky. When you get near the edge of the tower, you may need to reduce the brush size. Continue until the portion of the scratch that is in the sky is completely covered.

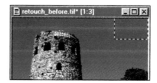

Figure 6.9 Photo after pasting the selection over the torn area.

Figure 6.10 The repair to the sky is successful.

Figure 6.11 When retouching, you should always enlarge the image when needed to provide a clear view of the flaw you are working on.

Figure 6.12 Selecting the area of sky to be copied with the Clone Brush.

Once the part of the scratch in the sky has been retouched, you can turn your attention to the scratch in the tower. The general technique is the same: right-click on the location in the tower whose pattern you want to copy, then paint the pattern over the scratch. I won't present steps for this task, as I am sure once you have mastered the procedure for the sky area you will be able to complete it with no problem. Remember, you may need to reset the clone brush's "seed" point and size as you work towards getting the best results.

Covering The Crayon Mark

The crayon mark looks like it can be covered using the copy and paste method that we used to retouch the tear in the sky. Because of the shape of the mark, and the shape of the background elements, it will be better to use the Freehand selection tool rather than the regular selection tool. Here are the steps you need to follow:

1. Enlarge the image so you can see the crayon mark and the surrounding area clearly.

2. Activate the Freehand tool. Be sure Feather is set to zero.

3. Draw a selection that includes part of the light path as well as part of the darker gravel next to the path (Figure 6.13).

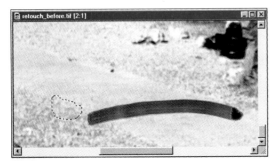

Figure 6.13   Selecting an area to paste over the left end of the crayon mark.

4. Press Ctrl+C to copy the selection, then Ctrl+E to paste it as a floating selection.

5. Move the floating selection until it covers the left end of the crayon mark. It is important that the edge of the path in the selection lines up properly with the edge of the path in the image. Left-click to drop the selection once it is positioned correctly (Figure 6.14).

Figure 6.14   Paste the selection so the edge of the path lines up.

6. Press Shift+N to remove the border from the selection.

7. Continuing with the Freehand tool, draw a selection in the path above the crayon mark (Figure 6.15).

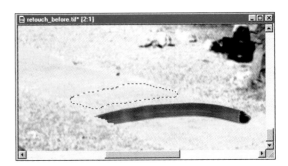

Figure 6.15   Defining a selection to paste over the central part of the crayon mark.

8. Press Ctrl+C then Ctrl+E to copy and paste the selection. Position and drop the selection over the crayon mark as described previously.

9. Continue with the copy/paste/position/drop procedure until you have completely covered the crayon mark.

When you are finished, zoom the image out to normal viewing size. You will be pleasantly surprised to find all traces of the flaws completely gone. The magic of digital retouching has rescued a photograph that otherwise would be headed for the trash.

Don't be discouraged if your first retouching attempts don't turn out perfectly. Remember, you are still learning! You can always return to the original image and start again. With a bit of practice you'll do just fine.

LOST SELECTION?

If the cursor is outside the image area when you press Ctrl+E to paste the floating selection, Paint Shop Pro will ask you if you want to delete the selection. Select No and continue.

Figure 6.16 After retouching, the image is flawless.

Before

After

Fixing Up Great Grand-Dad
Restoring an old photograph

One of the most rewarding retouching projects can be the restoration of an old photograph. Given that photography has been with us for well over 100 years, it is no surprise that millions of old photos are sitting in closets and drawers. Many of these photos represent priceless family memories and history. I know that it was quite an emotional experience for me to go through an album of photos from around 1920 showing my grandparents shortly after they were married, and my Dad as a young boy.

Unfortunately, many old photographs have suffered the ravages of time and mishandling. A beautiful old photograph may suffer from tears, stains, tape marks, and who knows what else. If the photograph was not properly processed or stored, chemical reactions in the paper can slowly destroy the image. There are therefore two reasons to use digital techniques for copying and restoring old photographs: to return the image to its original appearance (or as close to it as possible) and to preserve the image for the future.

Preparation

Before scanning an old photograph for digital processing, you can often perform some cleanup steps that will simplify the retouching that will be required. You must know what you are doing, and know what to avoid, or else you run the risk of causing additional damage. If you are in doubt, it is wise to do nothing rather than run the risk of ruining an irreplaceable photograph.

Black-and-white photographs, and most color photographs, can safely be washed to remove stains and other foreign material on the face of the photo. If the photo is permanently mounted to an album page with glue or tape, you may wish to soak the entire page rather than trying to separate the photograph from the page first. Use room temperature water in a clean, flat container, such as a non-stick baking pan. Immerse the photograph gently and let it soak for 5 or 10 minutes. Change the water if it becomes discolored, which can happen if there is water-soluble ink on the photograph or the page it is attached to. Stubborn deposits or stains that do not come out with soaking alone may yield to gentle rubbing with a ball of cotton. (I do mean gentle, as not everything can be removed by water and over-active rubbing can damage the photograph.)

After washing, hold the photo up by one corner to let most of the water drip off. Then, lay the photo face up on paper towels to dry. The photo may curl while drying. Once dry, you can flatten it by placing it under heavy books overnight.

Most old photographs will not require washing. It is advisable only in severe cases, but sometimes it can save an otherwise unsalvageable photo.

Scanning

Once the photograph has undergone any necessary preparation, the next step is scanning it into the computer. You learned the ins and outs of scanning in Chapter 3. If the photo is an old black-and-white image, take a close look at it. The image may not be truly "black" and white, but may have a brownish or sepia tone that once was popular. If you want to retain this tone in your digital copy, be sure to set your scanner to an appropriate color mode rather than to monochrome.

The Project

Now on to the project. Figure 6.17 shows a photograph of my great-grandfather that was taken around the turn of the century. The original photograph was trimmed to an oval shape and glued to a page in an album. Back then, black was the most popular color for pages in photo albums—hence the back background. In this project, I will take the photo of my great-grandfather and restore it.

> **BACKGROUND COLOR**
>
> When you create a new image from a non-rectangular selection, the areas of the image not covered by the selection will be filled with the current background color. For this project, I selected black as the background color before pasting.

Figure 6.17 An old photo of my great-grandfather, before being restored.

Figure 6.18 Selecting the oval area to be cropped.

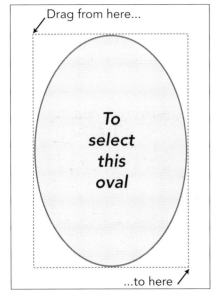

Figure 6.19 To select an oval area, drag diagonally across the imaginary enclosing rectangle.

Given the fact that this photograph is over 90 years old, it is in remarkable good shape. Even so, I can see several problems that can be repaired:

- The tears in the upper-right area
- The white lines that are visible in places around the edge
- The stain at the top
- A few white specks in the background behind the subject

The first step will be to crop the photograph. We will retain the oval shape, but by cropping just inside the current edge, we can get rid of the white lines and some of the tears. Here are the steps to follow:

1. Activate the Selection tool. On the style bar, choose Oval as the Selection Type. Be sure Feather is set to zero.

2. Select an area so that the boundary is just inside the edge of the photograph (Figure 6.18). Making an accurate oval selection is simplified if you imagine the rectangle the desired oval will just fit inside. Start dragging at one corner of this imaginary rectangle and drag to the diagonally opposite corner, as illustrated in Figure 6.19.

3. Press Ctrl+C to copy the selection to the clipboard, then Ctrl+V to paste it as a new image.

4. Save the original image, if necessary, then close it. Save the new image (Figure 6.20) under its own name.

The next things we will tackle are removing the stain at the top of the photo and repairing the tears. We will use the same tool, the Clone Brush, for both.

1. Use the Zoom tool to zoom in on the photo until the area of the stain is visible in detail.

2. Activate the Clone Brush tool. Use the style bar to set the tool options to Mode: Aligned; Size: 10; Shape: Round; Opacity: 128; Paper Texture: None.

3. Right-click in the image in the area to the right of the stain to select the "seed" point for the clone brush (Figure 6.21).

Figure 6.20 The cropped image.

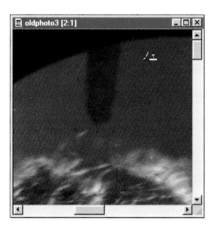

Figure 6.21 Selecting the seed point for the Clone Brush tool.

4. Paint over the stain to cover it with the same color as the unstained background. You may need several applications, and you may also need to select a different seed point.

5. If you mistakenly paint into the black background, right-click to select a black seed point and then paint over the mistake.

6. Use the scroll bars to scroll the image so the area with the tears is visible.

7. Still using the Clone Brush, select a seed point in the undamaged background near the tear, then paint over the tears until they are no longer visible. (I used the same Clone Brush settings as were used for the stain except for changing mode to Non-Aligned.)

8. When you have retouched the tears to your satisfaction, zoom out to see how the results look. Don't forget to save the image.

The final retouching task, and actually the easiest one, is getting rid of the white specks. There are a couple of specks in the background on the left side of the subject, and there is one on his lapel (see Figure 6.22).

Figure 6.22 Getting rid of the white specks on my great-grandfather's lapel is the next step.

Figure 6.23 Selecting an area to copy and paste over the white speck.

1. Use the Zoom tool to zoom in on the area of the lapel.

2. Activate the Selection tool. Set the tool options to Selection Type: Rectangle and Feather: 0.

3. Select a small area next to the speck (Figure 6.23).

4. Press Ctrl+C followed by Ctrl+E to copy the selection and paste it as a floating selection.

5. Move the selection over the speck, then left-click to drop it.

6. Press Shift+N to remove the selection border.

7. Scroll the image to bring the other specks into view. Use the same copy and paste techniques to cover up these specks.

That's it—we're finished. The final restored photograph is shown in Figure 6.24. An old, tattered album photograph now looks almost as good as the day it was made, over 90 years ago.

Figure 6.24 The final restored photograph.

It's true that some old photographs cannot be restored as success-fully as this one. Many photos are in much worse shape, and while digital retouching is a powerful technique, it cannot fix everything. Even if you cannot restore a valued photograph to like-new, you may still be able to improve it significantly.

Summing Up

Digital imaging has changed the retouching of photographs from a difficult and time-consuming chore to a simple task that almost anyone can master. Retouching jobs that used to be diffi-cult are now easy, and tasks that used to be impossible are now readily accomplished. Whether it's an antique photo of your forebears that is showing its age, or a brand new snapshot that someone set a coffee cup on, digital retouching skills are some-thing you'll often find useful.

FIXING 7 THE
BACKGROUND

Most photographs have a background—whatever is behind the main subject or subjects. While the background is secondary to the main subject, it can still be an important part of the picture. In fact, it is the background that often sets a terrific photo apart from an ordinary one.

Much of the problem with backgrounds stems from the fact that many photographers don't pay much attention to the background in their photos. This is understandable, because your attention is on the subject. I suggest you make an effort to be aware of your backgrounds. A little notice given to what's behind the subject can be one of the easiest ways to improve your photos. There are, of course, times when there is nothing you can do about the background when you're taking the photo. If, during your visit to Yellowstone Park, the sky behind Old Faithful is dull gray instead of bright blue, you may just have to live with it.

Or maybe not. With digital images, it is often possible to change a photograph's background. Chapter 1 presented some information on dealing with backgrounds when you take the photo. Here, we'll go more in-depth and discuss ways to manipulate a background to improve a photo.

Tools For Background Manipulation

You've already been introduced to many of the Paint Shop Pro tools you will be using to work with image backgrounds. Selections, copy and paste, brushes, and other image-manipulation tools can all be useful when you need to change a background. You learned how to use these tools in previous chapters; remember also that the Appendix includes an introduction to the basics of Paint Shop Pro. There's one more powerful tool, called *masks,* that is particularly useful for background work. Let's take a look at how to create and use masks before we get to the chapter's projects.

BLACK MASKS

When a mask is displayed for editing without the host image, it is always displayed in black and grays, even if the 50 % Red option is selected.

Photo courtesy of Maxine Okazaki

Figure 7.1   The original image of an orchid.

Using Masks

On Halloween, you wear a mask to cover your face. In Paint Shop Pro, a mask has a similar function—it covers something. In this case, the mask covers a digital image, or to be more precise, it covers part of the image. When you apply an action to the image, such as brightening it, only those areas that are not covered by the mask are affected by the action. Areas that are covered by the mask remain unchanged.

So far, a mask sounds pretty much like a stencil, which is just a piece of cardboard with shapes cut out of it. When you paint over the stencil, only the cutout areas are painted. Masks are more flexible,

however. While a stencil only has open and closed areas, a mask permits 256 different levels of "openness." A mask is actually a monochrome image with 256 levels of gray, ranging from black to white. Where the mask is black it is completely closed, where it is white it is completely open, and where it is gray you get an intermediate effect. Figures 7.1 and 7.2 show an example. Figure 7.1 is the original image, while Figure 7.2 shows a mask created for the image. This mask, which is black and white only (no grays) will permit image changes to only affect the orchid while leaving the background unaffected.

Figure 7.2 A mask created for Figure 7.1.

Figure 7.3 A mask can be viewed and edited while superimposed on the host image.

Viewing And Editing A Mask

A mask is always displayed and edited in the same window as the image with which it is associated (called the *host* image). You can view the image alone, the mask alone, or the mask superimposed on the image. Figure 7.3 shows the orchid photograph and its mask viewed together.

Two menu commands control the display and editing of the mask. On the Masks menu, the Edit command can be toggled on or off (but only if the current image has a mask):

- **Masks|Edit on**. The mask is displayed and editing actions affect the mask.

- **Masks|Edit off**. Editing actions affect the image. The mask may or may not be displayed, depending on the setting of the View|Thru Mask command.

The second mask-related command is the Thru Mask command on the View menu. This command is also an on/off toggle:

- **View|Thru Mask on**. The mask is displayed over the image. Editing affects either the mask or the image, depending on the setting of the Masks|Edit command.

- **View|Thru Mask off**. If Masks| Edit is on, the mask is displayed without the image and can be edited. If Masks|Edit is off, the image is displayed without the mask.

There are two options for viewing a mask and image together:

- The closed areas of the mask are black, the open areas are transparent, and intermediate areas are translucent gray, with darker grays corresponding to more closed areas of the mask.

- The closed areas of the mask are 50 percent translucent red, the open areas are transparent, and intermediate areas range from transparent to 50 percent red, with darker reds corresponding to more closed areas of the mask.

WHY USE MASKS INSTEAD OF SELECTIONS?

You may be thinking that you don't need to bother with masks because you can do the same things with selections. Not true! While selections limit image manipulations to the specified area, they do not permit the graduated effects that are possible with a mask. At best, using a selection is like using a black-and-white mask that has no shades of gray—adequate for some tasks, but often lacking the needed flexibility.

In addition, you have much more control over a mask. Because a mask is itself an image, you can use the full range of Paint Shop Pro's tools to manipulate it. For example, you can enlarge the view of a mask and edit it at the pixel level to ensure that the mask accurately follows the outline of some object in the image. Finally, the ability to create a mask from one image and apply it to another image provides capabilities that simply are not possible with selections.

In Figure 7.3, the mask is displayed with the red option. This setting has the advantage of having the image details visible even through the completely closed parts of the mask. This is useful if you are editing the mask based on the image contents. To set the mask display options:

1. Select Preferences from the File menu, then select General Program Preferences.

2. In the Preferences dialog box, click the Misc. tab.

3. Select either the 100% Black or 50% Red option.

4. Click on OK.

Creating A Mask

There are three ways to create a new mask for an image. Each is accessed by selecting Masks|New then selecting the corresponding command:

- **New**. Creates a new blank (solid black) mask that you can then edit.

- **From Image**. Creates a mask by converting an image to a 256-level gray scale image.

- **From Selection**. Creates a mask based on the selected area of the image. The selection becomes the clear part of the mask and the unselected area becomes the black part of the mask. This command is available only when the current image has a selection marked.

When creating a mask from an image, the image that the mask is created from does not have to be the host image. In fact, this is how you'll usually use this command, because creating a mask from the host image is rarely useful. You must have

open both the host image and the image from which the mask will be created. Then:

1. Make the host image active by clicking on its title bar.

2. Select New from the Masks menu, then select From Image. Paint Shop Pro displays the Add Mask From Image dialog box (Figure 7.4).

Figure 7.4 Creating an image mask from another image.

3. Pull down the Source Window list and select the image that you want the mask created from. To create the mask from the host image, select This Window.

4. Under Create Mask From select one of the following:

   - **Source Luminance**. The mask will be a gray scale copy of the image.

   - **Any Non-Zero Value**. Black areas in the source image will result in black areas in the mask. All other areas will be transparent in the mask.

5. Select the Invert Mask Data option to create a mask that is inverted—what would normally be black in the mask will be transparent, and so on.

6. Click on OK.

The source and host images do not need to be the same size. The mask will be stretched or compressed, if needed, to fit the host image.

Editing A Mask

Sometimes, you'll be able to create a mask that is just what you need without doing any editing. Other times, however, the mask will require modifications in order to perform the tasks you want to use it for. When editing a mask, it is easiest to simply think of it as a monochrome image—which is in fact exactly what it is. To put a mask in editing mode, select Edit from the Masks menu (or press Ctrl+K). You can then use all of Paint Shop Pro's image editing tools to modify the mask— Paint Brushes, Airbrush, Copy and Paste, brighten, contrast changes, and so forth.

You can invert a host image's mask by selecting Invert from the Masks menu. Select Delete from this menu to remove the mask.

Using A Mask

An image mask is "active" only when it is visible— that is, when the Through Mask command on the View menu is selected. When the mask is not active, image manipulation commands affect the entire image just as if there were no mask. To illustrate how a mask works, I will use the image shown in Figure 7.5. I created an empty mask for this image, then edited the mask to create a transparent rectangle and a middle gray rectangle within the black mask. The final mask is shown in Figure 7.6. Clearly this is not a mask that would be useful for any real task, but it provides a good demonstration.

Photo courtesy of Maxine Okazaki

Figure 7.5   The original image.

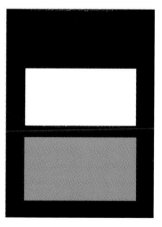

Figure 7.6   The mask created for the image in Figure 7.5.

SAVING AND LOADING MASKS

When you create a mask, it is saved along with its host image. You can also save the mask by itself. Once saved, a mask can later be loaded and applied to the same or a different host image. Saving masks can be very useful when you want to create more than one mask for a given host image, because an image can play host to only one mask at a time—in other words, an image can have only one mask. To save an image's current mask, select Masks|Save. To load a mask from disk and associate it with the current image, select Masks|Load. Masks are saved in files with the .msk extension.

You can also open a mask file directly, without a host image having to be open. Use the File|Open command to locate the .msk file and open it. You'll be able to manipulate the mask image just like any other 256-gray monochrome image.

WHERE'S MY MASK?

When you first create a mask, it will not be visible. Select View|Through Mask or press Ctrl+Alt+V to view the mask on the host image.

With the mask active, I then used the Colors|Adjust|Brightness/Contrast command to increase the image brightness by 45 percent. The resulting image is shown in Figure 7.7. You can see that where the mask was transparent the image was brightened the most, where the mask was gray it was brightened about half as much, and where the mask was black the image was not changed at all.

Figure 7.7   After applying 45 percent brightening through the mask.

Soft Focus!
Blurring the background

Figure 7.8 shows a photograph of my young friend Mr. Phillip Bruner. It's a very nice picture of Phillip, but the background leaves something to be desired. The patterns on the chair are slightly out of focus but still obvious enough to be distracting. The photo would be much nicer if the background were even more out of focus. By using a mask, we can blur the background while leaving Phillip untouched.

Before getting started, I will outline the procedures that we will use. First, we will define a selection that includes most of the area we want included in the mask. Because the subject's color and brightness values blend into the background in some places, such as his hair, it would not be possible to use the Magic Wand tool to define a selection that precisely follows the outline of the desired mask. Using the Magic Wand for the shirt and the Free-hand tool for the other areas, we can get reasonably close.

After creating a mask from the selection, the next task is to edit the mask so it accurately follows the outline of the subject. This will be somewhat time-consuming, but it can be easily accomplished using Paint Shop Pro's drawing tools.

Once the mask is in place and covering the subject, the final step is to apply a blurring filter to make the background appear more out of focus.

We will start by defining the selection and creating the preliminary mask.

1. Activate the Magic Wand tool. Set its options to Mode: RGB Value; Tolerance: 30; Feather: 0.

2. While holding down the Shift key, click on different areas of the shirt to create a selection that includes most of the shirt. Don't worry if the selection is not perfectly aligned with the edges of the shirt, or if there are small "islands" remaining unselected, we will fix that later.

Figure 7.8 The subject in the original photograph is fine, but the background needs improvement.

3. Activate the Freehand tool. Keeping the Shift key depressed, draw around the subject's head, keeping the line slightly inside the actual boundary. When you are finished, your selection should look something like Figure 7.9.

4. Select New from the Masks menu, then choose From Selection.

5. Press Ctrl+Alt+V to view the mask with the image.

6. You'll see that the mask is transparent over the area that was selected and solid over the background, which is the opposite of what we want. Select Invert from the Masks menu to reverse the mask areas. Your screen should now look like Figure 7.10 (assuming the 50% Red option is selected, as described earlier in the chapter).

Now we have a preliminary mask that covers most of the subject. It needs editing, however, to bring it in line with the edges of the subject. Here's what to do:

Figure 7.9 The selection on which the preliminary mask will be based.

Figure 7.10 The preliminary mask.

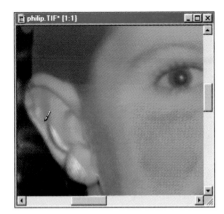

Figure 7.11 Extending the mask to the edges of the subject.

Figure 7.12 Viewing the mask without the image is useful to detect unwanted holes in the mask.

Figure 7.13 The finished mask accurately follows the outline of the subject.

1. Press Shift+N to remove the selection lines from the image.

2. Press Ctrl+K or select Edit from the Masks menu to put the mask in editing mode.

3. Using the Color Palette, set the foreground color to black and the background color to white.

4. Select the Paint Brushes tool. Set the options to Brush Type: Normal; Size: 20; Shape: Round; Paper Texture: None.

5. Paint using the left mouse button to extend the mask to the edges of the subject's shirt and face. For accurate painting near the edge, you should zoom in on the image (Figure 7.11). Change the brush size and shape as needed.

6. If you mistakenly extend the mask too far, hold down the right mouse button and "erase" the areas that go beyond the edges.

Press Ctrl+Alt+V now and then throughout the editing process to view the mask without the image (Figure 7.12). Viewing the mask this way makes it easy to find holes in the mask that need to be filled in, or places where the mask extends too far, that were not obvious when the mask was displayed over the image.

7. Once the mask is complete, press Ctrl+K to leave mask editing mode, then save the image. The finished mask is shown in Figure 7.13.

Now that we have the mask defined, the final step—blurring the background—is easy.

1. With the mask and image displayed together, as in Figure 7.13, select Normal Filters from the Image menu.

2. From the submenu, select one of the following:

   • **Blur**. Blurs the image slightly.

   • **Blur More**. Blurs the image by a greater amount.

   • **Soften**. Softens the image slightly.

   • **Soften More**. Softens the image by a greater amount.

3. Repeat Step 2 until you get the desired effect. For the example photograph, I used a combination of blurring and softening and applied each one several times.

4. When finished, save the image under a new name.

The image is finished, and Figure 7.14 shows the results. With the background thrown out of focus, the picture is much more pleasing.

Figure 7.14 With the background blurred, the photograph of Phillip is much improved.

Background Be Gone
Replacing the background

Some images have unattractive backgrounds that don't really lend themselves to improvement. Take the photo of my son Ben in Figure 7.15. The out-of-focus people in the background detract from the photo, but simply blurring them further would not help all that much. We could create a mask covering the subject and then darken the background to pure black, but the resulting image would look artificial. Perhaps the best solution is to replace the background altogether.

The techniques that we will use are similar to those used in Project 8. There's an added twist, however: In addition to using a selection to create a mask, we'll also use a mask to create a selection. Here's an outline of the procedure:

Figure 7.15 The background in this photograph should be replaced.

- Draw a selection that roughly follows the subject's edges.

- Create a mask from the selection.

- Edit the mask so it exactly matches the boundaries of the subject. (Up to this point, the procedures are the same as we used in Project 8.)

- Use the mask to create a selection whose boundaries exactly match the edge of the subject.

- Copy the selection and paste it onto a different image with a better background.

Of course, we will need a second image, the one that will become the new background. I selected the photograph in Figure 7.16. By itself it is a "mistake," an out-of-focus photo of trees. As a background, however, it will do quite nicely. Let's get started. Because the early steps in this project are the same as the previous project, I will not present as much detail as before.

Figure 7.16 This blurry image of trees will provide a good background.

1. Select the Freehand tool and create a selection that roughly follows the edges of Ben's head, face, and shirt (Figure 7.17).

Figure 7.17 The initial selection defines a rough outline of the subject.

2. Select New from the Masks menu, then select From Selection.

3. Press Ctrl+Alt+V to make the mask visible.

4. Press Shift+K or select Masks|Invert to invert the mask.

5. Press Shift+N to remove the selection border.

6. Press Ctrl+K to enter mask editing mode.

7. Use the Paint Brushes tool, as described earlier in this chapter, to fine-tune the mask so it exactly matches the border of the subject. When you are finished, the mask will look like Figure 7.18.

Figure 7.18 The finished mask exactly covers the subject.

At this point, we have completed a sequence of steps just like the ones we used in Project 8. The result is a mask that covers all of the subject and none of the background. Now we will do something different. We want to copy and paste the subject, but the Copy command does not recognize masks, but rather, requires a selection to copy only part of an image. The solution is to use the mask to define the selection, then use the selection to copy the subject. Here are the steps to follow:

1. Be sure the image is still in mask editing mode by pulling down the Masks menu and verifying that there is a checkmark displayed next to the Edit command.

2. Activate the Magic Wand tool. The option settings do not matter as long as Feather is set to 0.

3. Click anywhere on the red part of the mask. Because the image is in the mask editing mode, the Magic Wand will create a selection based on the mask image and not the original image. The selection border will fall exactly on the edge of the mask.

4. Press Ctrl+K to exit mask editing mode, then press Ctrl+Alt+V to hide the mask. You'll see that the selection border remains in place, but now defines a selection on the original image rather than on the mask (Figure 7.19).

Figure 7.19 After hiding the mask, the selection remains.

5. Press Ctrl+C to copy the selection to the clipboard.

6. Save the original image, then close it.

We have put Ben on the clipboard. Now we need the new background image to paste him into. Here are the steps to follow:

1. Open the background image, in this case the out-of-focus photo of the trees.

2. Press Ctrl+E to paste the selection from the clipboard as a floating selection in the background image. If you get an error message saying the selection is too big, follow the steps described in the next section.

3. Move the selection over the desired location on the image.

4. Click to drop the selection, then right-click to anchor it.

5. Save the final image under a new name.

Sometimes, when you try to paste the selection into the background image, you may get an error message that says "Clipboard object is larger than current image." This means that the selection you are pasting is too big to fit onto the image that you have selected for the background. If, for example, the selection is 1000×1500 pixels and the image is 900×1200, the selection simply won't fit. You can *resample* the destination image to increase its pixel dimensions. Here's how to do this:

1. Press Ctrl+V to paste the selection into a new image.

2. Press Shift+I to display the Image Information dialog box (Figure 7.20).

3. Note the selection's pixel dimensions, which are displayed along with other information in the dialog box. (In this case, the size is 1517×2191.)

4. Click on OK to close the dialog box, then close the image containing the selection without saving it—we only needed to determine its size.

5. Activate the background image by clicking on its title bar.

6. Press Shift+S to display the Resample dialog box (see Figure 7.21).

7. Change either the width or the height value to match or exceed the corresponding dimension of the selection that you noted earlier. These values are entered in the two boxes directly below the Custom Size option. If the Maintain Aspect Ratio box is checked, Paint Shop Pro will automatically change the other dimension (either width or height, depending on which one you changed) to retain the image's proportions. Both the width and the height dimensions of the destination image must be equal to or larger than the corresponding dimensions of the selection.

8. Click on OK. Paint Shop Pro will automatically convert the background image to the new pixel size.

ASPECT RATIO

This term refers to the image's width divided by its height. A perfectly square image, for example, has an aspect ratio of 1. By maintaining an image's aspect ratio when resampling it, you keep the original image proportions.

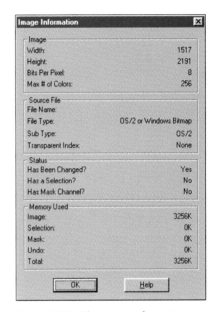

Figure 7.20 The Image Information dialog box.

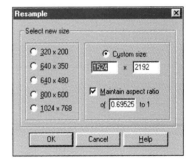

Figure 7.21 The Resample dialog box.

9. Continue with pasting the selection, as described earlier.

Figure 7.22 shows the final image after a bit of additional cropping. I think it is quite convincing. It would take close examination and a trained eye to detect that the image has been manipulated to change the background.

Figure 7.22 The final image looks as if the photograph was taken in a totally different location than the original.

When providing an image with a new background, the goal is to make the final image look as realistic as possible. Toward this goal, here are some tips to keep in mind:

- Use backgrounds with lots of detail, such as the trees used in this project. This kind of image works the best. If you try to use a background that is uniform, such as a clear sky, it is much more difficult to get the pasted subject to blend in realistically.

- Ensure that the subject and background have similar, if not identical, lighting. If the subject is in sunlight from the left but the sunlight is from the right in the background, the shadows pointing in different directions will be a sure giveaway that the image is a composite.

Changing The Weather
Improving the sky

PROJECT 10

The sky is one part of your photograph that you don't have any control over. If it's cloudy, then you're going to get a cloudy sky in your photo, period. Figure 7.23 is a good example. This photograph of the town hall in Siena, Italy, was taken on a day with a light overcast. The building is fine, but the gray sky is less attractive. I would have preferred a bright blue sky, and with digital manipulation, that's exactly what I will get.

Figure 7.23 An overcast sky gives a dull look to this photograph.

You might think that the easiest way to get a blue sky is to select the sky area and fill it with the desired color of blue. This is easy enough to do in Paint Shop Pro, but the result will look terrible. Even the smoothest of skies has some subtle variations in it, and an artificial sky that is a single, solid color will look just that—artificial. A better approach is to find another photograph that has a nice blue sky. The one we will use is shown in Figure 7.24. Taken in the Arizona desert, the main subject of this photograph is underexposed but, the blue sky is very nice—just what we need.

First, we will determine the required dimensions of the new sky image:

Figure 7.24 This photograph will provide the blue sky we need.

1. Open the image whose sky needs improvement—the town hall.

2. Press Shift+I to display the Image Information dialog box (shown earlier in Figure 7.20).

3. Make note of the pixel dimensions of the image (1524×2192 in this case), then click OK to close the dialog box.

Next, we will copy a section of blue sky into a new image:

1. Open the Arizona desert photograph—the image from which we are going to take the sky.

2. Using the Selection tool, select a rectangular region in a smooth area of the sky (see Figure 7.25).

3. Press Ctrl+C to copy the selection to the clipboard.

4. Close the Arizona desert image—we do not need it any more.

5. Press Ctrl+V. This will paste the selection into a new image by itself.

The next task is to resample the sky image we just created so that it is the same size as the original image of the town hall.

1. Press Shift+S to display the Resample dialog box. Enter the pixel dimensions that you copied earlier into the Custom Size boxes, but this time make sure the Maintain Aspect Ratio option is turned off. This will result in the resampled image of sky having the same aspect ratio, or height to width ratio, as the town hall image.

2. Click on OK.

We now have a uniform blue sky image that is exactly the same size as the town hall image. Before pasting the town hall over it, there is one more improvement we can make. You may have noticed in many photographs that the sky is lighter near the horizon than it is directly overhead. There seems to be a gradient of color with the sky, starting a lighter blue at the horizon and gradually changing to a darker blue overhead. We can use Paint Shop Pro's tools to imitate this effect in the photo. We will again turn to masks. Here's how:

1. With the blue sky image open, select Masks| New|Empty or press Ctrl+Y to create a new empty mask for the image.

2. Select Masks|Invert to invert the mask.

3. Press Ctrl+K to edit the mask. Because the mask has been inverted and the image is not displayed, all you'll see at this point is a blank white image.

4. Activate the Flood Fill tool and set its Fill Style option to Linear Gradient. Check the Color Palette to verify that the foreground color is black.

5. Click anywhere in the blank mask image. The image will be filled with a gradient starting with black at the bottom and fading to white at the top.

6. Select Invert from the Masks menu or press Shift+K to invert the mask so it is black at the top and white at the bottom. The mask will now look like Figure 7.26.

7. Press Ctrl+K to exit mask editing mode, then save the image. Remember, the mask is automatically saved with it.

Now that we have a gradient mask, we can selectively lighten the sky:

1. Press Ctrl+Alt+V to view the mask and the new image together.

Figure 7.25 Selecting the region of sky to be used.

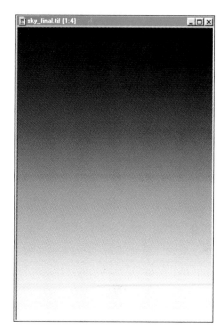

Figure 7.26 The gradient mask for the sky image.

Figure 7.27 Use the Brightness/Contrast dialog box to change the image brightness.

Figure 7.28 The sky image after applying brightening through the graduated mask.

Figure 7.29 Selecting the building for copying.

2. Press Shift+B to display the Brightness/Contrast dialog box (Figure 7.27).

3. Enter 40 in the % Brightness box and 0 in the % Contrast box, then click on OK to close the dialog box and apply the brightness change to the image. Because of the graduated mask, the brightness change will be applied to the image in a graduated fashion.

4. Press Ctrl+Alt+V to display the image without the mask. You can see that the sky image is now darkest at the top and lighter at the bottom (Figure 7.28).

Now it is time to copy the town hall from its original image and paste it over the sky we just created:

1. Make the town hall image active.

2. Select the Magic Wand tool. Set its Mode to RGB Value, Tolerance to 25, and Feather to 2.

3. While holding down the Shift key, click in the sky area as many times as needed to select the entire sky, including the small area of sky that is visible through the window at the middle right of the photo.

4. Select Invert from the Selections menu. The selection will now include all of the building and none of the sky (Figure 7.29).

5. Press Ctrl+C to copy the selected area to the clipboard.

6. Switch to the graduated sky image.

7. Press Ctrl+E to paste the selection.

8. Move the selection to the proper location, then click to drop it.

9. Save the image.

Congratulations! This has been the most involved project yet, but I think you'll agree that the results are worth it. As you can see in Figure 7.30, the scene in the photograph has been transformed from a gloomy gray day to a bright day with blue skies.

Figure 7.30 The final image with the beautiful sky.

Summing Up

Manipulating the background is one of the most effective ways
of changing (and improving) a photograph. In Paint Shop Pro,
selections and masks are two of the most useful tools for background work. In this chapter, the focus has been on realistic
background manipulations in which the goal is to make the
final image look like an original photograph that hasn't been
manipulated. Later in the book, we'll do some more fanciful
things with backgrounds.

PART 3

G E T
CREATIVE

COMBINING 8
PHOTOGRAPHS

One of the most interesting things you can do with digital imaging techniques is combine images—to create a final image that consists of multiple images combined in a creative and pleasing manner. The term *collage* is sometimes applied to this technique. You have already seen some basic applications of collage, such as in Chapter 7 when we cut a person out of one photo and pasted him into another. In that case, it was done to provide a more pleasant background. In this chapter, we will explore some more advanced ways to combine photographs using Paint Shop Pro.

Filling The Background

When you are creating a collage, you will sometimes need to create a background for the final image. This is not always necessary. In some collages, the entire final image consists of component photographs. When you do need to create a background, as we will in this chapter's first project, you'll find Paint Shop Pro's Flood Fill tool to be invaluable.

Think of the Flood Fill tool as a can of paint that can be filled not only with solid colors, but also with a variety of patterns. When you "pour" the paint onto an image, the color or pattern fills certain areas. You can control the areas that are filled by using selections or masks. Let's look at an example. Figure 8.1 shows the original image of skyscrapers in New York City. Figure 8.2 shows the result of using the Magic Wand to select the sky, then using the Flood Fill tool to fill the selection. It took me about 10 seconds to achieve this rather interesting effect.

Figure 8.1   The original image, taken in New York City.

Flood Fill Options

When the Flood Fill tool is active, the style bar displays the following tool settings:

- **Match Mode**. If set to None, the fill overwrites all pixels in the specified area (as controlled by the selection or mask). This option can also be set to RGB Value, Hue, or Luminance, which cause the fill to overwrite only pixels that match the spot you click.

- **Tolerance**. If Match Mode is set to RGB Value, Hue, or Luminance, specifies how closely a pixel must match the seed pixel to be filled. Has no effect if Match Mode is None.

Figure 8.2 The Flood Fill tool converts an unexceptional image into something that catches the eye.

- **Fill Style**. Specifies the type of fill. You can use a solid color, one of several gradients, or a user-defined pattern. Gradients and patterns are explained in the next section.

- **Options**. If Fill Style is set to anything other than Solid, clicking the Options button opens a dialog box where you set additional options for the specified style.

If Fill Style is set to Solid Color, then the fill uses the foreground color or the background color, depending on whether you click with the left or right mouse button.

Using Fill Gradients

Paint Shop Pro offers four geometrical gradient fills: Linear, Radial, Rectangular, and Sunburst, as illustrated in Figure 8.3. Each fill combines the current foreground and background colors, fading from one to the other in the pattern specified by the fill.

CREATING FILL PATTERNS

You can often create attractive fill patterns by selecting part of a photograph, copying it to a new image, then reducing its contrast and/or increasing its brightness.

Figure 8.3 From left to right, Linear, Radial, Rectangular, and Sunburst fill gradients created with the Flood Fill tool.

In Figure 8.3, the Linear fill was done with Black as the background color, while the other fills were done with White as the background color.

Each of the gradient fills has option settings that control the orientation and placement of the fill. These options are set by clicking the Options button on the style bar. Figure 8.4 shows the options dialog box for the Linear gradient fill, which permits you to set the direction of the gradient. The options for the other gradient styles are equally obvious and you should have no problem figuring them out.

Figure 8.4 The Gradient Fill Direction dialog box showing options for the Linear fill.

Using Fill Patterns

Some very nice effects can be obtained with user-defined fill patterns. You can use all or part of any image as a pattern when using the Flood Fill tool. First, open the image that contains the pattern you want to use. You can also select part of the image at this time. Figure 8.5 shows an example.

Figure 8.5 The image with the area selected that is to be used for the pattern.

Next, activate the Flood Fill tool and select Pattern as the Fill Style setting. Click on the Options button to display the Define New Pattern dialog box. Pull down the New Pattern Source list and select the source image. The preview in the dialog box will show the selected pattern (Figure 8.6).

Figure 8.6 The selected area previewed in the Define New Pattern dialog box.

Click on OK to close the dialog box. Now you can use the Flood Fill tool to fill areas with this pattern. Figure 8.7 shows an image that was filled with the pattern selected in Figure 8.6.

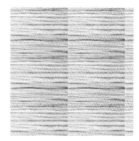

Figure 8.7 This image is filled with the pattern selected in Figure 8.6.

PROJECT 11

Turning Three Into One
Creating a collage

The term *collage* refers to an image that is created by combining two or more images. When you were a kid, you probably made collages from magazine photos using scissors and paste. But with digital technology, the possibilities are much wider. In this project, I'll show you how I combined the three photos of my son, Ben, shown in Figure 8.8 to make a collage. This was a big hit with the grandparents.

The first step is to rotate the two photos that will go at the left and right side of the collage.

Figure 8.8 The three original photos.

1. Open the first image.

2. Select Rotate from the Image menu to display the Rotate dialog box (Figure 8.9).

3. Under Direction, select Left. Under Degrees, select Free, and enter 10 in the box.

4. Click on OK. The image will be rotated by the specified amount (Figure 8.10).

5. Open the second image and repeat Steps 1 through 4. This time rotate the image 10 degrees to the right.

6. Save both rotated images under new names.

WORKING WITH MULTIPLE AND LARGE IMAGES

Working with collages is one area where you are likely to find yourself using multiple images and very large images. This sort of work puts severe demands on your computer's random access memory, or RAM. In Windows 95, if there is not sufficient RAM, information is saved to disk in a temporary *swap file*, which acts as a kind of auxiliary memory. While a swap file works fine, it slows things down a lot because direct access to RAM is hundreds of times faster than access to disk. Here are a few tips to minimize delays when working with multiple large images.

• Make sure all other applications are closed when working in Paint Shop Pro.

• Have only necessary images open. For example, if you are copying a selection from one image to another: First, copy the selection to the clipboard; then, close the first image; next, open the second image; and finally, paste the selection.

• If there is a large selection on the clipboard and you will not need to paste it again, use the Empty Clipboard command on the Edit menu to delete the data from the clipboard. This frees up memory that is then available for other purposes.

• Be sure there is a enough free space—at least 100MB, preferably more—on the disk drive used for the swap file. (This is almost always drive C.)

• Use the Disk Defragmenter to keep the swap file disk optimized. You will usually find this program, which is part of Windows 95, on the Start|Programs|Accessories|System Tools menu.

Even with these precautions, operations with large images can be slow—even on a fast computer system with lots of RAM. Don't be surprised if saving an image, or copying a large selection to the clipboard, takes several minutes. Paint Shop Pro is designed to work with large images and you shouldn't have any problems other than the inconvenience of waiting.

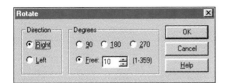

Figure 8.9 The Rotate dialog box.

Figure 8.10 After rotating the image 10 degrees to the left.

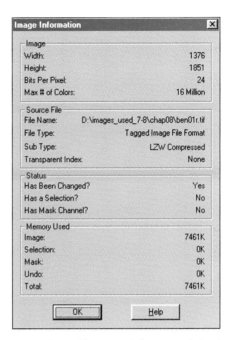

Figure 8.11 The Image Information dialog box provides information on the current image.

Next, we'll create a new image into which we will assemble the collage. We need to know the size required, which depends on the sizes of the images that will go into the collage. Here's what to do:

1. Activate one of the rotated images, then select Image Info from the View menu, or press Shift+I, to display the Image Information dialog box (Figure 8.11).

2. Make note of the image's width and height—in this case, 1376×1851. The second rotated image will have the same size, so we do not need to specifically measure it.

3. Open the middle image, which is the one that will not be rotated. Use the Image Information dialog box to make note of its

dimensions. In this example, the dimensions are 1096×1684.

4. Calculate the minimum width needed: 1376 + 1376 + 1096 = 3848.

5. Since the images will be positioned horizontally, the minimum height needed is the height of the tallest image: 1684.

6. We have a minimum size for the new image of 3848×1684. We will need to increase this to allow for space between and around the images. I settled on the final size of 4404×2212.

7. Select New from the File menu to display the New Image dialog box (Figure 8.12).

8. Enter the calculated dimensions in the Width and Height boxes. Be sure that Background Color is set to White and Image Type is set to 16.7 Million Colors (24 bit).

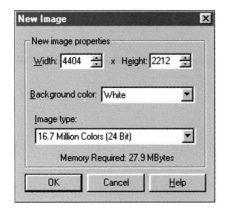

Figure 8.12 Specifying the dimensions of the new image.

9. Click on OK. A new, blank image of the specified size will be displayed.

Now we must paste each of the three original images into the blank image that we just created.

1. If necessary, open the image that was rotated to the left and make it active.

2. Press Ctrl+C to copy the entire image to the clipboard.

3. Make the collage image active and position the mouse point anywhere on it.

4. Press Ctrl+E to paste the clipboard image as a floating selection.

5. Move the mouse until the floating selection is at the desired position, then click to drop it.

6. Repeat Steps 1 through 5 with the other two images. When you are done, the collage will look like Figure 8.13. Don't forget to save the collage to disk. You can close the three original images at this time.

So far, so good. But the white background is not particularly attractive. Our next task will be to do something about it. In order to prevent our actions from affecting the images as well as the background, we will create a mask. You learned the details of working with masks in Chapter 7, so I will not go into great detail here.

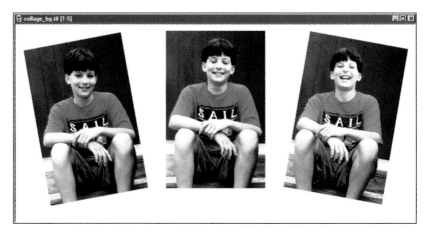

Figure 8.13 The collage after pasting the three images.

1. With the collage displayed, select the Magic Wand tool. Set its options to Match Mode: RGB Value; Tolerance: 0; Feather: 0.

2. Click anywhere in the white background. The Magic Wand will define a selection that includes just the background. This operation may take a moment or two as it is a large image. When the selection borders are displayed, do not worry if they do not exactly follow the edges of the images because we will have a chance to edit the mask later.

3. Select New from the Masks menu, then select From Selection. A mask will be created that covers only the areas of the image outside the selection (that is, the three photos).

4. Press Ctrl+Alt+V to make the mask visible. The image will now look like Figure 8.14.

BLACK MASK?

If your mask displays as solid black instead of the transparent red shown in Figure 8.14, you need to change a Paint Shop Pro option. Select Preferences from the File menu, then select General Program Preferences. In the dialog box, click the Misc. tab, then select the 50% Red option.

Figure 8.14 The mask created to cover the three images.

5. Check the mask to be sure its borders accurately follow the edges of the three images. The one place where you may have problems is the sunlit wood behind the subject. If you find mistakes, press Ctrl+K to enter mask editing mode, then use the techniques you learned in Chapter 7 to correct the mask.

6. When the mask is correct, press Ctrl+K again to exit mask editing mode, then save the image.

Now that the mask is in place, we are ready to create the background. By using a mask to cover the three images, we will be able to apply a color or pattern to the image and have it affect only the background. We will use the Flood Fill tool to create a background. You learned the details of using this tool earlier in the chapter, so I will present only the basic steps here.

1. Display the collage image with its mask, as was shown earlier in Figure 8.14.

2. Using the Color Palette, select a medium blue as the foreground color and white as the background color.

3. Make the Flood Fill tool active. On the style bar, set the tool options as follows: Match Mode: None; Fill Style: Radial Gradient.

4. Click the Options button on the style bar to display the Gradient Fill Origin dialog box (Figure 8.15). Use this slider to set Vertical to 24% and Horizontal to 50%, then click on OK.

5. Click anywhere in the collage. Paint Shop Pro will fill the background with the selected radial gradient fill. This operation may take a few moments. When it is complete, press Ctrl+Alt+V to hide the mask. Your image will look like Figure 8.16.

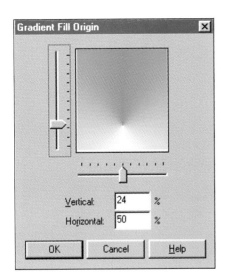

Figure 8.15 The Gradient Fill Origin dialog box.

Figure 8.16 The collage after applying a radial gradient fill to the background.

Looks pretty good, doesn't it? However, you will probably notice that there are some white spots or lines along the edges of the three photographs, where the background fill did not reach. This is not because you did something wrong, but is simply an un-avoidable consequence of the way masks and fills operate. We can easily hide these distracting marks by drawing a frame around each photo.

1. Select the foreground color that you want to use for the frame. I used the same blue as was used for the background fill.

2. Make the Line tool active. On the style bar, set Width to 10.

3. Draw a line along each edge of all three photographs. After drawing each line, carefully examine the image to ensure that the line is exactly where you want it. If it is not, press Ctrl+Z to undo the line, and then redraw it.

4. When all lines have been drawn, save the image.

The collage is complete, and the final image is shown in Figure 8.17. We have taken three attractive, but ordinary photographs, and created something that is a bit out of the ordinary. Just one example of the many interesting things you can do with collages.

Figure 8.17 The final collage combines the three photographs into a single, attractive image.

PROJECT **12**

The Wider, The Better
Creating a panorama

A *panorama* is a view that is wider than usual, such as you might see from the edge of the Grand Canyon or the top of the Empire State Building. When you take a photograph of such a view, you may find the results disappointing because a single photo cannot take in the breadth and majesty of the scene. Professional photographers resort to specialized and expensive equipment to capture panoramic images, but you don't have to. With the magic of digital manipulation, you can create a panoramic photograph using your regular camera.

The trick is to take several photographs of the scene, turning slightly between shots to frame a different part of the view. Later, use Paint Shop Pro to stitch the individual photographs into a single panorama. If you use reasonable care when taking the original photographs, you can create striking panoramas where it's hard to tell where one photo ends and another begins.

When taking the photos that will be made into a panorama, it's important to keep the camera as level as possible. In other words, the camera should be pointing straight ahead, and neither up nor down. If you don't do this, things that are vertical in the scene—trees, for example—will not be vertical in the photograph unless they happen to be dead center. This makes it difficult or impossible when putting the panorama together to create a good match between the right edge of one photo and the left edge of another.

For perfect matches between photographs, you'll need to use a tripod. With a carpenter's level, adjust the tripod so that its head is perfectly level. Attach the camera, and frame each shot by rotating the tripod head. While this method is cumbersome, it is the best way I know to make sure the edges of the photographs match up perfectly. Fortunately, there's rarely a need to use a tripod. By paying attention, you should be able to hand-hold the camera level enough. You won't get a mathematically perfect match, but the mismatch will usually not be noticeable.

It's also important to overlap your photographs. There's no way you are going to end one photo exactly where the next one starts. By overlapping, you guarantee that there are no gaps in the panorama. You don't want to overlap photos too much, of course. Here's how I ensure a reasonable amount of overlap when taking photos for a panorama: When I'm framing the first photo, I'll notice some object that's just inside one edge of the photo. When I turn to frame the second photo, I'll make sure that object is just inside the opposite edge of the image.

Now let's get to our panorama project. Figure 8.18 shows a series of four photographs I took in Arizona's Monument Valley. I took these photos with the intention of creating a panorama. I think you'll agree that the panoramic image is a lot more effective at communicating the grandeur of the desert landscape.

Figure 8.18 The four individual photos that will go into the panorama.

To create the panorama, the first step is to determine the size of the image that will be needed.

1. Open the first image.

2. Select Image Information from the View menu, or press Shift+I, to view the Image Information dialog box. You saw this dialog box earlier in Figure 8.11.

3. Make note of the image's dimensions—for this image, it's 1596×2320.

4. Click on OK to close the dialog box.

The other three images will have the same dimension, so we do not need to check them individually. We will be combining the four images horizontally, so you might calculate the width of the final image as 4×1596 = 6384. Because there will be some

overlap from one image to the next, however, the final image will not need to be quite this wide. Let's try a width of 5000.

For image height, we could simply use the height of the original images. There may be some slight vertical offset between images, so it's a good idea to add a little extra room. We'll use 1750. Now, to create the new image:

1. Select New from the File menu to display the New Image dialog box (shown in Figure 8.19).

2. Enter the image dimensions that we calculated in the Width and Height boxes.

3. Be sure that Image Type is set to 16.7 Million Colors and Background Color is set to White.

4. Click on OK. Paint Shop Pro will create and display a new, blank image.

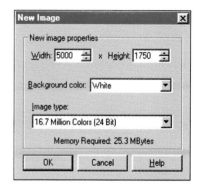

Figure 8.19 Specifying the dimensions of the new image in the New Image dialog box.

We are now ready to begin copying the individual images to the new image and positioning them. Because you will be working with multiple large images, you should heed the suggestions presented in the sidebar, "Working With Multiple And Large Images:"

1. Make the first image active.

2. Press Ctrl+C to copy the entire image to the clipboard.

3. Close the first image, and make the new, blank image active.

4. Press Ctrl+E to paste the first image as a floating selection.

5. Use the mouse to position the selection against the left side of the image, midway between the top and bottom edges, then click to drop it.

6. Open the second image.

7. Repeat Steps 2 through 4 to paste the second image into the new image.

8. Position the selection so its left edge matches the subject matter in the existing image, then click to drop it.

9. Press Shift+N to remove the selection border. Your screen will look like Figure 8.20.

Figure 8.20 The panorama after positioning the first two photos.

10. Repeat Steps 6 through 9 with the third and fourth images.

All the parts of the panorama are now in place. You'll notice, however, that the top and bottom edges of the image are not straight because the vertical alignment of the component photos was not perfect. This is easily fixed:

1. Activate the Selection tool.

2. Define a rectangular selection that includes only the parts of the image that you want included in the final version, trimming off the jagged edges.

3. Press Ctrl+C to copy the selection to the clipboard.

4. Close the original panorama image.

5. Press Ctrl+V to paste the selection as a new image.

6. Save the new and final panorama image under a new name.

Figure 8.21   The final panorama.

Figure 8.21 shows the final panorama. I think it looks pretty good, and believe me, it looks even better when displayed at a larger size.

If you look closely at the final image, you may notice that the color and brightness match between the edges of the component photographs is not perfect in all spots. You would think that images taken from the same location only seconds apart would be perfectly matched, and in many cases they are. This problem arises from time to time because of certain cameras' automatic exposure systems, which may give each individual photograph in the panorama series a slightly different exposure.

If your camera has the capability to set exposure manually, or to lock the exposure, I suggest using this feature to ensure all of the photos for a panorama are taken with exactly the same exposure. You can also use Paint Shop Pro to manipulate the brightness and/or color balance of the individual photographs to make them match before putting them together into the final image. In many cases, however, the minor mismatches will not be noticeable under normal viewing.

Summing Up

Creating collages and panoramas is one of the most popular ways that people make use of the flexibility of digital photography. These techniques often require you to work with multiple large images, which can tax your computer and your patience. The results, however, are usually well worth the hassle.

TEXT IN
9
PHOTOGRAPHS

Figure 9.1 I created a nice title image by adding text to this image.

It has been said that a picture is worth a thousand words. But sometimes a picture is worth even more—if it has a few words in it. You'll find plenty of opportunities to use text in your digital images, whether it be to create a title image for your slide show, add a catalog number to a product shot, or design a greeting card. Figure 9.1 is a good example of how text can improve an image, showing the title shot I created for the photos of a trip to Spain. Paint Shop Pro provides all the text capabilities you need for just about any project. In this chapter, I'll show you how to add text to images as well as how you can use images to make your own custom text.

The Text Tool

Anything you do with text in Paint Shop Pro will involve the Text tool. Using it is easy—simply select the tool, then click in the image at the location where you want the text. Paint Shop Pro displays the Add Text dialog box, as shown in Figure 9.2.

There are several parts to this dialog box. In the Font Attributes section, you select the appearance of the text:

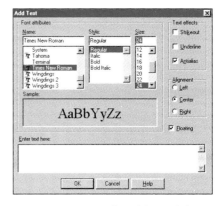

Figure 9.2 You use the Add Text dialog box to put text in your images.

- **Name**. Specifies the font of the text, which determines the appearance of the individual letters. This list will display the names of all the fonts installed on your system.

- **Style**. Lets you choose among normal text, boldfaced text, italicized text, or text that is both boldfaced and italicized.

- **Size**. Specifies the vertical size of the text, expressed in *points*. A point is $1/_{72}$ of an inch. If you do not see the exact point size you want in the list, you can enter it directly in the Size box.

- **Sample**. Shows the exact appearance of the font with the attributes you have selected.

The Text Effects section lets you add one or more effects:

- **Strikeout**. Displays the text with a line through it, as shown in Figure 9.3.

~~Struck out text appears like this~~

Figure 9.3 Struck out text.

- **Underline**. Displays the text with underlining, as shown in Figure 9.4.

<u>Underlined text appears like this</u>

Figure 9.4 Underlined text.

- **Antialias**. Softens jagged character edges by using shades of the text's color. This effect is available only for images in 256 gray scale mode and for color depths greater than 256.

The Alignment option determines how the text is aligned. This option affects only text with more than one line:

- **Left**. The left edges of the lines are aligned.

TEXT POSITION

The Alignment option does not control where the text is placed relative to the spot you clicked with the Text tool. The text is always centered on that point regardless of the Alignment option setting.

- **Center**. The centers of the lines are aligned.

- **Right**. The right edges of the lines are aligned.

The Floating option controls how the text is added to the image. When the Floating option is on, text is added in the current foreground color as a floating selection. Like any other floating selection, you then use the mouse to position the text, and click to drop it. When Floating is off, text is added as a selection with no color of its own. You can then use the usual methods of working with selections to fill it; for example, with a pattern using the Flood Fill tool.

Finally, Enter Text Here is where you type the text that you want to add. Use the standard editing keys to edit the text; press Enter to start a new line. When finished, click on OK to close the dialog box and add the text to the image.

Rotating Text

Text that you add to an image is always oriented horizontally, at least originally. Before you "drop" the selection, you can use the Rotate command to rotate the text to any desired orientation by following these steps:

Figure 9.5   The Rotate dialog box lets you rotate text that you are adding to an image.

1. Select Image|Rotate, or press Ctrl+R, to display the Rotate dialog box (Figure 9.5).

2. Under Direction, select the direction you want the text to rotate: Right (clockwise) or Left (counterclockwise).

3. Under Degrees, select one of the preset rotation amounts: 90 (one-quarter turn), 180 (one-half turn), or 270 (three-quarters turn). Or, select Free and enter the desired degrees of rotation in the box.

4. Click on OK. The selection is rotated by the specified amount.

Other Text Effects

Because text you add with the Text tool is initially retained as a selection, you can apply just about all of Paint Shop Pro's editing tools and special effects to the text before making it a permanent part of the image. There are two approaches to using special effects with text:

- Add the text directly to the destination image. While the text is still a floating selection, apply the special effects. When done, drop the text onto the image.

- Add the text to a new, blank image. Apply the special effects to this image, then copy the text and paste it into the final image.

Which method you use will depend on the specific effect you are using. The first is the easiest, but it does not work well in all cases. For example, placing the text in a separate image will make it easier to evaluate the appearance of the effects you are applying. Once you have the effect you want, you can then copy the text to the final image.

TRANSPARENT SELECTIONS

When you create text in a separate image to be pasted into another image, you want to paste it as a *transparent* selection. When you paste a transparent selection, only the text is visible—the background is transparent and lets the background image show through. Figure 9.6 shows some text that was placed in its own image.

Figure 9.6 The original text.

Figure 9.7 shows that text pasted into another image as a regular selection, and Figure 9.8 shows the same text pasted as a transparent selection.

Figure 9.7 An image with the text pasted as a regular selection.

Here's how to create text and paste it as a transparent selection:

1. Use the File|New command to create a new, blank image large enough to hold the text. Make the background color of the new image White.

2. Add the text to this image, and apply any desired special effects to it.

3. Use the Color Palette to ensure that the current background color is white—the same as the background color that was used when creating the new image.

4. Use the Selection tool to define the selection around the text you want to copy, then press Ctrl+C to copy the selection to the clipboard.

5. Make the destination image active.

6. Select Edit|Paste|As Transparent Selection, or press Ctrl+Shift+E, to paste the text into the image.

7. Position the text to the desired location, then click to drop it.

Figure 9.8 An image with the text pasted as a transparent selection.

Giving Credit Where Credit Is Due

PROJECT **13**

Creating a title shot

Titles shots and credits—we have all sat through them at the movies. And even though they may seem boring at times, they often serve a useful purpose. If you're creating an on-screen slide show, for example, you should let the viewers know exactly what they are looking at. Is it pictures of your vacation to Iceland or a demonstration of a new fire extinguisher? Also, you may want to give yourself and anyone else who contributed to the project credit, so the viewers will know whom to thank (or blame).

This project will show you how to create an attractive title shot. We will use the photograph in Figure 9.9 as an introduction to a show titled the Gardens of England. Rather than just plopping some text into the image, we will be a little more creative. You can see that the final effect is to have the colored text surrounded by a thin border of white, which provides a more attractive and easy-to-read title.

Figure 9.9   The image that will be used for the title shot.

The first task is to create the white "cutout" where the text will be placed.

1. Make the Text Tool active, and click in the exact center of the image horizontally and a bit above the center vertically.

What's a Feather?

When you feather a selection, you expand it by blurring the borders. The greater the feathering, the more blurry the selection's borders are.

2. In the Add Text dialog box, select Tahoma font, Regular style, and enter 90 in the Size box. Select the Antialias and Center options, and be sure that the Floating option is turned off. If you do not have this font on your system, select another font whose appearance you like.

3. In the Enter Text Here box, type "Gardens of England," pressing Enter after the "Gardens" and also after "of."

4. Click on OK. The text will be added as a selection border to the image, as shown in Figure 9.10.

Figure 9.10 The title text added as a defined selection.

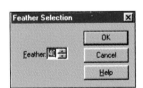

Figure 9.11 The Feather Selection dialog box.

5. Select Modify from the Selections menu, then select Feather. The Feather Selection dialog box is displayed (Figure 9.11).

6. Enter 40 in the Feather box, then click on OK. You'll see that the selection borders in the image expand by the indicated amount.

7. Select Masks|New|From Selection to create a mask based on the selection (in other words, in the shape of the text). Press Ctrl+Alt+V to view the mask along with the image, and press Shift+N to hide the selection borders. If the mask displays as solid black rather than transparent red, select File|Preferences|General Program Preferences; then, on the

Misc. tab, select the 50% Red option. Note that the mask covers all areas of the image outside the text. Press Shift+K to invert the mask. Your image will now look like Figure 9.12.

8. Press Ctrl+K to enter mask editing mode, then press Ctrl+Alt+V to hide the image. You'll see only the mask, in black, on your screen.

9. Select Image|Normal Filters|Blur More to blur the edges of the mask. Select this command two or three times to get the desired degree of edge blurring (I did it twice). Your mask will look like Figure 9.13.

10. Press Ctrl+K to exit mask editing mode.

11. Press Ctrl+Alt+V to display the image along with the mask.

12. Press Shift+K to invert the mask again. The mask will now cover all areas of the image except the text.

13. Activate the Flood Fill tool. Set its Fill Style to Solid Color and its Match Mode to None. The Tolerance setting does not apply when Match Mode is set to None.

14. Use the Color Palette to select white as the foreground color.

15. Click in any area not covered by the mask. The unmasked areas will be filled with white.

16. Press Ctrl+Alt+V to hide the mask. The image will now look like Figure 9.14. Save the image under a new name.

Figure 9.12 After defining a mask to cover the text.

Figure 9.13 The mask after blurring its edges.

Figure 9.14 The image after filling the unmasked areas with white to provide a cutout for the text.

Now that we have created the white cutout that will serve as the background for the text, it's time to add the text itself.

1. Use the Color Palette to select the desired foreground color for the text. I used a blue with an RGB value of 5,25,255.

2. Activate the Text tool, and click near the center of the image.

3. Turn on the Floating option in the Add Text dialog box. You'll notice the text and options have not changed.

4. Click on OK. The text will be placed in the image as a floating selection.

5. Position the text over the white cutout area. You want a thin border of white showing around each letter in the text.

6. Click to drop the text, then right-click to hide the selection borders. Don't forget to save the image.

Our title image is complete. Figure 9.15 shows the final result. It looks like a thoroughly professional job to me. That white border is the touch that differentiates this title from the ordinary.

Figure 9.15   The final title slide.

Fancy Text
Creating text from an image

So far, we have been talking about putting text into images. What about creating text *from* an image? Using this method, you can create elaborate and fancy letters that have many uses. Generally, you'll find that creating text from an image works best when the text is relatively large. With small text and thin letters, the image pattern will usually not show up to good advantage.

In this project, we'll explore two techniques: creating text from a geometric pattern and creating text from a photograph.

Creating Text From A Geometric Pattern

To create text from a pattern, you have at your disposal all of Paint Shop Pro's tools for creating interesting designs. Perhaps the most useful tool is the Flood Fill tool, which lets you fill entire images, or parts of them, with a variety of patterns. You learned how to use this tool in Chapter 8, so I will not repeat the details here. Let's get to work.

1. Select New from the File menu to display the New Image dialog box. Create an image that is 600 pixels wide and 100 pixels high, with a white background and 16.7 million color image type.

2. Use the Color Palette to select white as the background color and a bright purple as the foreground color.

3. Make the Flood Fill tool active and set its Fill Style option to Linear Gradient.

4. Click on the Options button on the style bar to display the Gradient Fill Direction dialog box. Enter 0 in the Deg box, then click on OK.

5. Click anywhere in the blank image. The resulting gradient is shown in Figure 9.16.

Figure 9.16 The gradient from which the text will be created.

6. Select the Text tool, then click in the center of the gradient image. The Add Text dialog box will be displayed, as shown earlier in Figure 9.2.

7. Select the desired font and options. I used Tahoma normal at 72 points. Be sure that the Floating option is turned off.

8. Enter the desired text in the Enter Text Here box. For this example, I entered "WAY TO GO!"

9. Click on OK. The text outline appears as a selection border in the gradient image, as seen in Figure 9.17.

Figure 9.17 The text as a selection in the gradient image.

10. Press Ctrl+C to copy the selection to the clipboard.

11. Switch to the image where you want to insert the text. For this demonstration, I created a new image, 600×100 pixels with a black background.

12. Press Ctrl+E to paste the selection. Position the text to its desired location, then click to drop it.

Figure 9.18 shows the result. The text created from the linear gradient is a lot more attractive than if we had simply created text in a solid color. You can experiment with Paint Shop Pro's other fill types to obtain a wide variety of text effects.

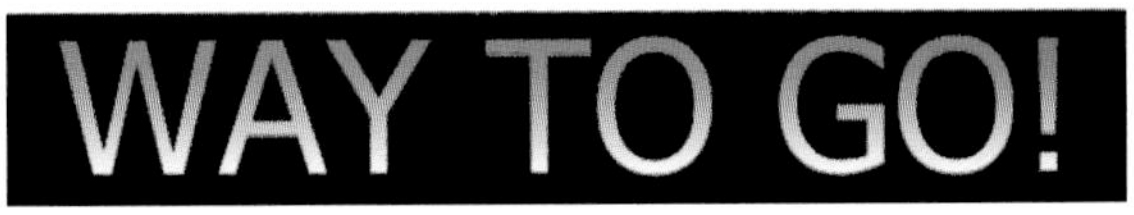

WAY TO GO!

Figure 9.18 The resulting text.

Creating Text From A Photograph

You can achieve some very interesting effects by actually creating text from a photo. The procedure is not much different from that used to create text from a pattern. Let's see how the text in Figure 9.16 was created. The original image is shown in Figure 9.19.

Figure 9.19 The photograph that we will use to create text.

1. With the source image open, activate the Text tool and click in the middle of the image. Paint Shop Pro will display the Add Text dialog box.

2. Select the desired font and options. I used MS Sans Serif bold at 90 points. Be sure that the Floating option is turned off.

3. Enter the text "TOMATOES" in the Enter Text Here box, then click on OK. The text outline will display as a selection border (Figure 9.20).

Figure 9.20 The text as a selection border in the original image.

4. Press Ctrl+C to copy the selection to the clip-board.

5. Use the Color Palette to select a light green as the background color.

6. Select New from the File menu to display the New Image dialog box. Create a new image that is 700×150 pixels. Open the Background Color drop-down list and select Background Color.

7. Click on OK. You will see a new image that is filled with the light green background color you selected.

8. Press Ctrl+E to paste the selection from the clipboard. Position it, then click to drop it.

The final image is shown in Figure 9.21. I can't think of a more effective way to say "tomatoes." You can use this method to create text from any image, and the possibilities are limited only by your imagination.

Figure 9.21 The completed "tomatoes" image.

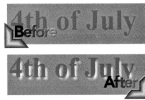

PROJECT
15

Drop It!
Text with drop shadows

There are plenty of other text effects you can create with Paint Shop Pro. One of the most useful is to add a drop shadow, starting with the text shown in Figure 9.22. By following these steps, it took about two minutes to create this text.

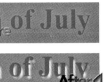

Figure 9.22 After adding the text as a floating selection.

1. Select File|New to display the New Image dialog box. Create a new image that is 320×90 pixels with red as the background color.

2. Use the Color Palette to select blue as the foreground color.

3. Activate the Text tool, then click in the middle of the image.

4. In the Add Text dialog box, select Times New Roman, Bold, 48 points. Make sure that the Floating option is turned on. Enter "4th of July" in the Enter Text Here box.

5. Click on OK. The text will be added as a floating selection. Position the text in the upper left of the image. Do not right-click to drop the selection, since we need it to remain defined as a selection for the next step. Your image will look like Figure 9.22.

6. Select Special Effects from the Image menu, then select Add Drop Shadow. Paint Shop Pro will display the Drop Shadow dialog box (Figure 9.23).

7. In the Attributes section of the dialog box, specify white as the color, 255 as the Opacity, and 20 as the Blur.

8. For Offset, specify 6 for both Vertical and Horizontal.

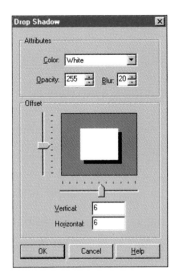

Figure 9.23 You specify drop shadow settings in the Drop Shadow dialog box.

9. Click on OK and the shadow will be added to the image. Press Shift+N to remove the selection borders. The final image is shown in Figure 9.24. Remember to save the image to disk.

Figure 9.24   Text with a drop shadow can add impact.

The 4th of July image is just one example of the many things you can do with text in Paint Shop Pro.

Summing Up

You'll probably find that relatively few of your images require text, but when the need arises, it's nice to know that Paint Shop Pro has the tools you need. Remember that once text has been inserted into an image, it is simply a part of the image and has no special characteristics. You can use any and all of Paint Shop Pro's tools to make it look just the way you want. Whether it's plain text or fancy text, you have the freedom to display it just the way you want.

SPECIAL
EFFECTS,
PART 1

10

We all know that special effects add pizzazz to many of the movies we watch, but did you know that special effects can also be used to spice up your digital images? Paint Shop Pro offers a variety of effects that let you modify color, perspective, and other image characteristics. We'll learn how to use some of these effects in this chapter and Chapter 11.

How do special effects differ from the other manipulations that you can do with Paint Shop Pro? In the earlier chapters, our digital manipulations were aimed at producing a final result that looked natural, as if it had not been manipulated at all. With special effects, there is no attempt to retain the natural, unmanipulated look. Rather you are changing the image in order to obtain a special and dramatic appearance—in other words, a special effect. Figures 10.1 and 10.2 show an example of what I'm talking about. Special effects called *posterizing* and *solarizing* were used to convert the photograph of the fish pond into the dramatic painting-like image in Figure 10.2.

Figure 10.1 The original photograph of a fish pond.

Figure 10.2 Special effects converted an ordinary photo into this unusual image.

Techniques For Special Effects

Before getting to the projects, let's take a look at some of the
special effects that Paint Shop Pro offers. You will use these techniques, either alone or in combination, to achieve different final
results. We won't be using all of these techniques in the projects,
but you will want to experiment with them on your own.

Posterizing

As you may have already guessed, the posterize function makes
an image look like a poster. But what exactly does that mean?
Think about the appearance of posters you have seen, such as
movie advertisements. Particularly in older posters, the image
uses a lot fewer colors than a photograph. A tree, for example,
will be only two or three shades of green instead of the hundreds
of shades you'd see in a realistic photograph. This is how
posterizing works—it reduces the number of colors in an image.

You can apply different levels of posterizing by specifying the number of bits per color. As you learned earlier in Chapter 1, a digital photograph uses 8 bits of information to represent the level of each of the three primary colors (red, green, and blue). Thus, each primary can have 2^8 or 256 different levels, and the three primaries together can represent 256×256×256 or more than 16 million colors. The posterize function reduces the bits per color to a value between 1 and 7. Table 10.1 gives the colors available at each posterization setting.

Figure 10.3 The Posterize dialog box.

To posterize an image:

1. Select the region to be posterized. If there is no selection, the effect will be applied to the entire image.

2. Press Shift+Z or select Posterize from the Colors menu to display the Posterize dialog box (Figure 10.3).

3. Enter the number of bits per color in the Bits Per Channel box, or click the up and down arrows to change the value.

4. The thumbnail image in the dialog box shows the appearance of the current setting. Click on the Preview button to temporarily apply the effect to the image.

5. Click on OK to accept the setting and posterize the image.

Posterizing with bits per channel settings of 7, 6, or 5 is not too interesting because the effects are quite subtle. A setting of 4 bits per channel usually provides a noticeable effect, and lower settings provide very dramatic results. Figure 10.4 shows the effects of different levels of posterizing.

Table 10.1 Results of different posterize settings.

Bits per color	Levels of each primary color	Total colors
7	128	approximately 2 million
6	64	262,144
5	32	32,768
4	16	4,096
3	8	512
2	4	64
1	2	8

Figure 10.4   The original image on the left followed by posterized versions at 4, 2, and 1 bit per channel.

Solarizing

The term *solarize* originated with a technique that is used with photographic film. It was discovered that if a photo was grossly overexposed, some of the brightest areas would "invert" and become dark. This effect was caused by a photochemical reaction in the film, and because sunlight was often used to produce the overexposure, the process became known as solarizing.

Solarizing in Paint Shop Pro has a similar effect, but it works not only with brightness, but also with colors. Select Colors|Solarize to display the Solarize dialog box (Figure 10.5). Enter the luminance threshold, in the range 1 through 254, in the Threshold box. Pixels whose luminance is above this threshold will have their colors inverted, while other pixels will not be changed. Lower threshold settings result in more of the image being solarized.

Figure 10.5   Set the solarization threshold in the Solarize dialog box.

What exactly does it mean to "invert" a color? It is a simple formula applied to the pixel's RGB value:

new red value = 255 - old red value

new green value = 255 - old green value

new blue value = 255 - old blue value

For example, white (255,255,255) becomes black (0,0,0), blue (0,0,255) becomes yellow (255,255,0), and so on. Figure 10.6 illustrates the effects of solarizing at thresholds of 50 and 200.

Negative Image

The Negative Image command on the Colors menu inverts all colors in the image. It is like solarizing the image with a threshold of 0. If you invert an image twice, the result is identical to the original image.

Figure 10.6 The original image (top) was solarized with threshold levels of 50 (center) and 200 (bottom).

Arch Impact
Creating a concept poster

The goal of this project is to create a visually striking poster to promote the concept of arches. I had a very nice photograph of the arches in a medieval German monastery, but the photo lacked the kind of impact that I wanted. I thought that the posterize function in Paint Shop Pro might provide the desired result.

Here are the steps required to create the concept poster.

1. Load the original image into Paint Shop Pro.

2. Press Shift+Z to display the Posterize dialog box (shown earlier in Figure 10.3).

3. Enter 2 in the Bits Per Channel box, then click on OK.

4. Use the Color Palette to select white as the foreground color.

5. Select the Text tool, then click near the bottom of the image. Paint Shop Pro will display the Add Text dialog box (Figure 10.8).

Figure 10.7   The original photograph has plenty of arches but lacks impact.

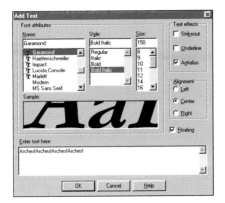

Figure 10.8 The Add Text dialog box.

6. Select Garamond as the Name and Bold Italic as the Style. Enter 150 in the Size box. Be sure that the Antialias and Floating options are selected.

7. Enter the text "Arches!Arches!Arches! Arches!" in the Enter Text Here box.

8. Click on the OK button. The dialog box will close and the text will be added to the image as a floating selection.

9. Use the mouse to position the text, then click to drop it.

10. Press Shift+N to remove the selection borders.

11. Save the image under a new name.

In a few easy steps, we have transformed an ordinary photograph into an eye-catching poster. The final result is shown in Figure 10.9. Posterizing emphasizes the shapes of the arches in the photograph while hiding irrelevant details, exactly the effect we wanted.

Figure 10.9 The final poster.

Bring Out The Picasso In You
Making a photo look like a painting

I have always wished I could be a skilled painter. I have tried my hand at watercolors and oils, but have never produced anything I was tempted to keep. Fortunately, my urge to create "paintings" is at least partially fulfilled by the power of digital image manipulation. Using the tools of Paint Shop Pro, it is possible to convert a photograph into an image that looks like a painting. I'll show you how in this project.

Just as there are many different styles of painting, there are various manipulations that can make an image look less like a photograph and more like a painting. You should not consider the steps presented in this project to be a fixed recipe that can be successfully applied to any photo. You can use them as a starting point for your own experiments. It helps to think about the ways that paintings usually differ from photographs. Here are some of the more important ways in which paintings usually differ from photographs:

- The image is not as sharp; fewer details are visible.

- Fewer colors are used.

- Brush strokes are visible in the image.

- The texture of the paper or canvas shows through.

Keep these differences in mind as you select the digital manipulation tools to use.

Now let's get to the project. This project has two parts, one dealing with a landscape and the other with a portrait.

Painting A Landscape

The original photograph is shown in Figure 10.10. This brilliant aspen tree was photographed in a canyon in Arizona. While I like the photograph, I felt that applying a painting-like effect might create a more interesting image.

Figure 10.10 The original photograph.

The techniques I used to achieve this effect were:

- Resample the image at a lower resolution to reduce detail.

- Posterize at a bits per channel value of 3 to reduce the number of colors.

- Apply an edge enhancement filter to suggest brush strokes.

- Use the Clone Brush to add a canvas texture.

Here are the steps to follow:

1. Load the original image.

2. Press Shift+S to open the Resample dialog box (Figure 10.11). Select Custom size and enter 200 in the left of the two boxes (the Width box). Be sure that the Maintain Aspect Ratio option is on, and the proper height of 302 will automatically be placed in the other box.

Figure 10.11 Resampling the image to a lower resolution.

3. Click on OK. The image will be resampled to the specified pixel dimensions. It will be displayed at a very small size, so you will need to press the + key on the numeric keypad a few times to zoom in.

4. Press Shift+Z to open the Posterize dialog box (shown earlier in Figure 10.3).

5. Enter 3 in the Bits per Channel box, then click on OK. The posterized image is shown in Figure 10.12.

6. Select Edge Filters from the Image menu, then select Edge Enhance. This filter processes the image to emphasize edges. Figure 10.13 shows the result of applying this filter.

7. Press Ctrl+C to copy the image to the clipboard, press Ctrl+V to paste it as a new image, then press Del to erase the image. This is a quick and easy way to create a new, empty image that is the same size and color depth as the one you are working on.

8. Activate the Clone Brush tool. On the style bar, set the tool options as follows: Clone Mode: Aligned; Size: 100; Shape; Round: Opacity: 128; Paper Texture: Coarse Canvas.

9. Click the title bar of the original image to activate it, then right-click in the image to specify the seed point for the clone brush. When you do so, look at the left end of the status bar and note the pixel coordinates of the spot you click.

10. Click the title bar of the new blank image. With the Clone Brush tool still active, move the mouse pointer to the same coordinates in the blank image.

11. Press and hold the left mouse button, and start painting. Continue painting to clone the entire image. Figure 10.14 shows the partially completed image.

Figure 10.12   The image after resampling and posterizing.

Figure 10.13   After applying the edge enhance filter.

Figure 10.14 "Copying" the image with the Clone Brush.

12. When the copying is complete, save the new image under its own name. Close the original image without saving it so the original image of the tree will remain unchanged.

Voilà! Your masterpiece is complete. A person who is not familiar with digital manipulation techniques would have no idea that the image in Figure 10.15 originated in a camera.

Figure 10.15 The completed "painting."

Painting A Portrait

Portraits are a popular subject for both photographs and paintings. Painting effects can be particularly attractive in portraits, and the result is often more flattering than the original photograph. In this project, I'll show you a quick and easy way to convert a photographic portrait to a painting-like image. The image we will use is shown in Figure 10.16. This photograph of my daughter Claire, taken when she was quite young, seemed like a good candidate for conversion to a "portrait."

Figure 10.16 The original photograph of Claire.

As you'll see, the steps required to achieve this effect are rather simple:

1. Load the original image.

2. Press Shift+S to open the Resample dialog box.

3. Select Custom Size, and enter 100 in the first box. With the Maintain Aspect Ratio option selected, the Height setting will be automatically set to 83.

4. Click on OK. The image will be resampled to the extremely low pixel resolution, and will be displayed at a small size.

Figure 10.17 After resampling to a low pixel resolution, individual pixels are visible in the image.

Press + a few times to zoom in. You'll see that the individual pixels are visible in the image (Figure 10.17).

5. Press Shift+S to open the Resample dialog box again. This time, resample to a resolution near the original one. I used 1600×1312. By resampling back to a high resolution, we maintain the appearance of pixels in the image while obtaining the high resolution required for high-quality reproduction.

6. Select Normal Filters from the Image menu, then select Blur More. This command will soften the edges of the "pixels" in the image. If you want more blurring, increase the effect by selecting Image, Normal Filters, Soften More.

7. Select Image, Special Filters, Add Noise. In the dialog box, select the Random option and enter 20 in the % Noise box, then click on OK.

8. Save the image under a new name.

We're finished. The final image is shown in Figure 10.18. Easy to apply manipulations such as these provide you with a wealth of creative opportunities.

Figure 10.18 The completed portrait.

Summing Up

Paint Shop Pro provides dozens of special effects for you to use on your images. Because you can combine two, three, or even more effects on a single image, the creative possibilities are practically endless. You've learned how to use a few effects in this chapter's projects, and we will look at some more in the next chapter.

SPECIAL
EFFECTS,
PART 2

11

You may be wondering how many digital special effects are possible with Paint Shop Pro. I have asked myself the same question, and the only answer I have been able to come up with is: "a heck of a lot." Start with the fact that there are dozens of different image manipulation commands, and many of them have one or more options that can be set one way or another. Then consider that you may apply two, three, four, or even a dozen different manipulations to an image between start and finish. The number of different combinations seems almost endless. There's no way I can show you even a small fraction of the possibilities. At best, I can introduce you to a few of the available techniques and hopefully whet your interest so you will explore further on your own.

Other Color Models

Throughout this book, we have been working with the RGB color model, in which the colors of an image are defined by the intensities of the three primary colors: red, green, and blue. There are two other color models that you need to be familiar with.

The HSL Color Model

HSL stands for hue, saturation, and luminance. In this model, a color is defined by three numbers that specify (you guessed it) its hue, saturation, and luminance:

- **Hue.** This perceived color is commonly expressed by color names, such as red and purple. In the HSL model, hue is specified by a number between 0 and 360. This number represents the position of the color, in degrees, on the standard color wheel. Figure 11.1 shows the color wheel stretched out to rectangular form. You can see that the colors on the wheel start at red, run through green and blue, then return to red. Paint Shop Pro uses the values 0 through 255 to represent the full range of hues, rather than 0 to 360.

Figure 11.1 The hue values in the HSL color model range from 0 on the left to 360 (255 in Paint Shop Pro) on the right.

- **Saturation.** This is a number between 0 and 255 that specifies the color's purity. A saturation setting of 255 gives the purest and brightest color, while a setting of 0 gives gray regardless of the hue.

- **Luminance.** This is the brightness of the color, ranging from 0 to 100. A luminance setting of 0 is always black, and a setting of 100 is always white.

> **HSB?**
>
> The HSL model is sometimes called the HSB model, where the B stands for brightness.

Paint Shop Pro does not use the HSL model when adjusting or creating colors, but you need to be familiar with it when using the Colorize function, which is described later in this chapter.

The CMYK Model

There is one other color model you should be aware of, even though Paint Shop Pro does not support or use it at all. In the CMYK model, the first three letters stand for the subtractive primary colors: cyan, magenta, and yellow. The subtractive primaries, you will remember from our discussion in Chapter 5, are used when colors are created with paints or inks. Before images are printed, therefore, they are converted to this model so that the values can be used to control the amount of ink applied to the paper.

The K in CMYK stands for black. Even though, in theory, a mixture of cyan, magenta, and yellow will produce black, the qualities of printing inks are such that a true black cannot be obtained this way. Hence, high-quality printing uses four colors of ink—the three subtractive primaries plus black. This means that in a CMYK image, each pixel is represented by four numbers, which give the relative values of these four components.

Paint Shop Pro does not let you use CMYK mode directly. However, when you print a color image on a color printer, the image is converted to this mode as it is sent to the printer. More advanced image manipulation programs, such as

Adobe Photoshop, support an on-screen CMYK mode that permits you to precisely tune the printed appearance of your images. This level of accuracy is rarely needed except in professional printing applications.

Creating Monochrome Images

You can obtain some very interesting results by converting an image, or part of it, to *monochrome*. As the name suggests, a monochrome image has only one color. A black-and-white photo is perhaps the most common example of a monochrome image, and we all see them every day in newspapers and magazines.

You may ask: But aren't these images really two colors—black and white? I suppose you could look at it that way, but in black-and-white printed images the white is simply the paper, so only one color of ink is needed to print them. Hence, the term monochrome.

Why would you want a monochrome image? Color is such an important part of many images that it may seem odd to get rid of it. There's no doubt, however, that monochrome images can be very beautiful and are sometimes more effective than color at communicating an idea or emotion. In a world that is flooded with color images, it is sometimes the monochrome photograph that stands out from the crowd. Paint Shop Pro offers two commands for converting color images to monochrome: Grey Scale and Colorize.

The Grey Scale Command

The Grey Scale command, located on the Color menu, converts a color image to gray scale. Each pixel in the image is converted to a shade of gray that is equivalent to its luminance. There are 256 possible shades of gray, ranging from 0 (black) to 255 (white). There are no settings or options for this command. The Grey Scale command makes the photograph look as if it had been taken with black-and-white film.

The Colorize Command

The Colorize command is somewhat more flexible than the Grey Scale command. It coverts an image to a uniform hue and saturation while retaining the original luminance. The effect is like converting a color photo to black and white and then tinting it with a single color. Technically, these are two color images because they contain both black and the tint color, but they are generally grouped together with true monochrome images. To colorize an image, press Shift+L, or select Colors|Colorize, to display the Colorize dialog box (Figure 11.2). Enter the desired hue and saturation values in the appropriate boxes. Click on the Preview button to see the effects of the settings on the image, and click on OK to close the dialog box.

Figure 11.2   The Colorize dialog box.

Figure 11.3 shows some examples of colorizing an image. The original image is on the left, the middle image was colorized with a hue of 0 and a saturation of 100, and the image on the right used a hue of 180 and a saturation of 255.

Figure 11.3   The original image and two colorized versions of it.

REPLACING COLORS

Paint Shop Pro's Color Replacer tool makes it possible to replace one or more colors in an image with a new color. While not used in this chapter's projects, it is a useful tool and you should know the basics of how it works. You start by using the Color Palette to select the colors; the tool will replace the background color with the foreground color. It is most convenient to use the Eyedropper tool to select the colors by left- or right-clicking in the image to select the foreground or background color, respectively.

The Color Replacer has a Tolerance setting that specifies how closely a color must match the background color to be replaced. A setting of 0 requires an exact match, while larger values will replace colors that are within the specified tolerance of the background color.

There are two ways to use the Color Replacer: You can double-click in the image to replace all pixels in the image or selection (if one is defined). Or, you can "paint" to replace colors only in certain areas. In this case, the Color Replacer works much like the Paint Brushes tool and you have the same options: Size, Shape, and Paper Texture.

Applying Deformations

As the name suggests, Paint Shop Pro's deformation commands change the image by deforming it in some way. Some of the deformations are geometrical, such as the Circle deformation, which makes the photo look like it has been stretched over the surface of a ball (Figure 11.4.). Other deformations alter the appearance of an image by moving pixels from one location to another. For example, the Motion Blur deformation makes an image look like it is in rapid motion by blurring it in a specified direction.

There are two ways to apply a deformation to an image (or a selected area of an image). If you know the deformation that you want, all you need to do is select Image|Deformations, then select the desired command from the submenu. Some deformations have no options and are applied immediately, while others will display a dialog box where you can set options. As with other Paint Shop Pro commands, these dialog boxes all have a Preview button that lets you see the result before actually applying the deformation.

If you are not sure which deformation you need, select Image|Deformation Browser. The Deformation Browser dialog box displays a list of available deformations and a sample preview that shows what the selected deformation looks like (Figure 11.5). Once you have chosen the desired deformation, click on Apply.

Figure 11.4 Before and after applying the Circle deformation.

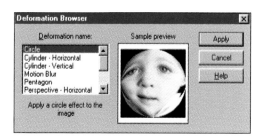

Figure 11.5 The Deformation Browser dialog box.

PROJECT 18 **Aging Gracefully**
Making a photograph look
"old fashioned"

There is a certain charm to old photographs, an appeal that can be difficult to achieve with modern photographic techniques. What is it about old photos that makes them special? Of course the subject is important, as is the style of dress and other factors that say "old." In a 100-year-old photograph of your great-great-grandfather, for example, his high starched collar and handlebar mustache are part of the picture's charm. Other aspects of old photographs have to do with the photographic techniques that were used. Black and white was the only option available, and some of the old techniques resulted in photos with a warm, brown tint.

How, then, can we take a modern photograph that was created with a digital camera (or scanned from a color print) and give it that "old fashioned" look? Here are some tips:

- Choose an appropriate subject. A picture of someone wearing a Grateful Dead T-shirt is not going to look old no matter how you manipulate it.

- If your photo is in color, use the Grey Scale command to convert it to black and white.

- Use the Colorize command to apply a brown tint to the image.

Let's get started with the project. We will turn the perfectly modern photograph in Figure 11.6 into an image that looks as if it could have been taken 100 years ago.

1. Load the original image into Paint Shop Pro.

2. Select Colors|Colorize, or press Shift+L, to display the Colorize dialog box (shown earlier in Figure 11.2).

3. Enter 17 in the Hue box and 170 in the Saturation box, then click Preview to see how the image will look if you use these settings.

Figure 11.6 The original image of a young child.

4. Adjust the Hue and Saturation settings if desired. Decreasing the Hue value will make the image warmer (more red) while increasing the value will make it cooler (less red).

5. When you have the desired hue and saturation settings, click on OK.

6. Activate the Selection tool. In the style bar, set Selection Type to Ellipse and Feather to 5.

7. Draw a selection to include the part of the picture that you want in the final image (see Figure 11.7).

Figure 11.7   Selecting the area to copy.

8. Press Ctrl+C to copy the selection to the clipboard, then press Ctrl+V to paste it as a new image (see Figure 11.8).

9. Make the original image active, then select File|Close. When asked to save the image, select No. This leaves the original color image unchanged on disk.

Figure 11.8   The selected area pasted as a new image.

10. Activate the Magic Wand tool. On the style bar, set its Match Mode to RGB Value, Tolerance to 10, and Feather to 5.

11. Click in one of the white areas of the image. If the selection that the Magic Wand creates does not include all four of the corner white areas, hold down the Shift key and click in the unselected white areas. The goal is to create a selection that includes all of the white areas.

12. Activate the Flood Fill tool. On the style bar, set Fill Style to Solid Color. The settings of the other options do not matter.

13. Use the Color Palette to set the foreground color to black.

14. Click in one of the white areas. The black fill may extend to all of the white areas with one click, or you may have to click several times.

15. When completed, save the image.

The final image is shown in Figure 11.9. Note the thin white border between the oval image and the black background. This is the result of using a Feather setting of 5 when we copied the image and also when we defined the background selection. Other settings would result in a larger border, or none at all. While this is really a photo of my daughter, who's to say it isn't really a picture of my great-grandmother as a child?

Figure 11.9 The final image.

Figure 11.10   *The original photograph of the Cape Hatteras lighthouse.*

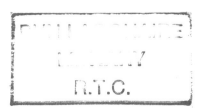

Boss Man
Embossing techniques

PROJECT 19

The technique of embossing involves stamping a piece of paper or metal so that the design stands out from the surface. You can achieve a similar effect with Paint Shop Pro's emboss filter. This filter suppresses the colors in the image and outlines the edges with black and white. The result is that many of the details in the image are removed, and it has the "raised" look that real embossing achieves. It can be useful for converting photographs into design elements in which the main shapes in the image are emphasized.

For this project, I started with the photograph in Figure 11.10. To be honest, this is not a particularly impressive photo. The image is not as sharp as it could be, and the colors are washed out. Nevertheless, it will serve perfectly as the starting point for this project. In the final image, you can see that the colors and details have been removed, and only the shapes remain. Anyone who has been to the North Carolina coast would know instantly what this is.

Let's first apply the emboss filter.

1. Open the original image in Paint Shop Pro.

2. Press Shift+B to open the Brightness/Contrast dialog box (Figure 11.11).

3. Enter 33 in the Contrast box, and 0 in the Brightness box. Then click on OK. This increase in contrast will make it easier for the emboss filter to find the edges in the image.

Figure 11.11 The Brightness/Contrast dialog box.

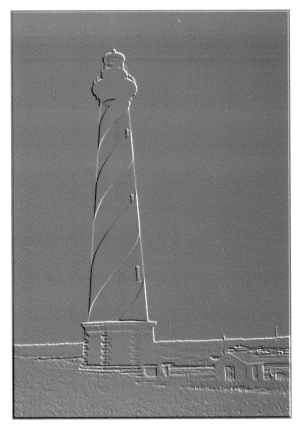

Figure 11.13 The final embossed lighthouse image.

Figure 11.12 The image after applying the Emboss filter.

6. Enter 160 for Hue and 80 for Saturation, then click on OK.

7. Save the final image under a new name.

4. Select Image|Special Filters|Emboss. Paint Shop Pro will apply the emboss filter and the image will look like Figure 11.12. If we wanted a gray image we could stop here. Let's continue, however, and give the embossed image some color.

5. Press Shift+L to open the Colorize dialog box (shown earlier in Figure 11.2).

The final image is shown in Figure 11.13. With this project, we have completely transformed the original image. From an ordinary photograph of a lighthouse, we have created a simplified image that retains only the most important elements of the subject's shape and pattern. There are plenty of uses for images such as this. For example, the owner of Lighthouse Bait and Tackle might find it just right for his Web page logo.

Over The Edge
Working with edge filters

PROJECT **20**

Every images contains edges, where a bright area is next to a dark area or one color is adjacent to another. Paint Shop Pro offers several filters that manipulate edges in an image, and we will use them in this project to create a strange and surrealistic image from a photograph of a mask. The original image is shown in Figure 11.14.

Figure 11.14   The original photograph.

The first step will be to even out the image brightness. Notice how the original image of the mask is brighter toward the top as a result of the illumination coming from above. The edge filters work better if an image has even brightness.

1. Press Shift+Y, or select Masks|New|Empty, to create a new, empty mask for the image.

2. Press Ctrl+K to view and edit the mask. At this stage, the mask will be solid black.

3. Make the Flood Fill tool active. On the style bar, set the Fill Style to Linear Gradient.

4. Click on the Options button to display the Gradient Fill Direction dialog box (Figure 11.15).

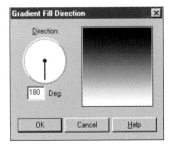

Figure 11.15 the Gradient Fill Direction dialog box.

5. Enter 180 in the Deg box, or use the mouse to move the pointer in the Direction circle to point straight down, then click on OK.

6. Use the Color Palette to select black and white as the foreground and background colors, respectively.

7. Click anywhere in the mask image to create the linear gradient mask shown in Figure 11.16.

Figure 11.16 The gradient image mask.

With the image mask that we have created, we can brighten the image and have the change affect the bottom part of the image more than the top, resulting in an image that has even brightness from top to bottom. We will also increase the contrast of the image to enhance its edges, which will improve the performance of the edge filters that we will apply later.

1. Press Ctrl+K to exit mask editing mode. If the mask is not visible on top of the image, press Ctrl+Alt+V to display it (see Figure 11.17).

Figure 11.17 The image displayed along with the gradient mask.

2. Press Shift+B to display the Brightness/Contrast dialog box (shown earlier in Figure 11.11). Enter 30 in the % Brightness box and 0 in the % Contrast box, then click on OK.

3. Select Masks|Delete to delete the image mask, as we do not need it any more.

4. Press Shift+B to open the Brightness/Contrast dialog box again.

5. Enter 0 in the % Brightness box and 80 in the % Contrast box, then click on OK. We now have a high-contrast image of the mask with even brightness (Figure 11.18). Save the image under a new name.

Figure 11.18 The mask photograph after adjusting brightness and contrast.

Our next task is to do some minor retouching of the image. Note the dark shadow under the mask's chin. If we apply edge filters to the image as it is now, the edges of the shadow will be picked up just like the "real" edges, and the resulting image will not look as good. To avoid this problem we will copy another part of the image and paste it over the shadow to fill in the missing details.

1. Activate the Selection tool and select a rectangular area at the top edge of the mask, as shown in Figure 11.19.

2. Press Ctrl+C to copy the selection to the clipboard, then press Ctrl+V to copy it into a new image.

3. Select Image|Flip to invert the new image (Figure 11.20).

4. Press Ctrl+C to copy the inverted image to the clipboard.

5. Make the original image active, then press Ctrl+E to paste the selection.

6. Move the selection until it is positioned over the shadow below the mask's chin, with the mask edges aligned. Left-click to drop the selection, then right-click to remove its borders. The image will now look like Figure 11.21. The temporary image that holds the selection can be closed without saving.

Figure 11.19 The area to be copied has been selected.

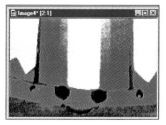

Figure 11.20 The copied area of the image after it was inverted.

Figure 11.21 The image after pasting the selection over the shadow.

Figure 11.22 After defining a selection to include the shadowed areas.

I will not claim that the image looks realistic at this point—the pasted section under the chin is quite obvious—but for the purpose of this project, this will not matter. While we have taken care of the shadow below the chin, there are still shadows to the sides of the chin that need some attention. Also, the pasted rectangle extends a bit outside the oval outline of the mask, and we need to trim this excess off.

1. Make the Magic Wand tool active. Set Match Mode to RGB Value, Tolerance to 50, and Feather to 0.

2. Hold down the Shift key and repeatedly click in the shadow areas at the sides of the chin. This will define a selection that encompasses the entire shadow (see Figure 11.22).

3. Activate the Eyedropper tool.

4. Click on a yellow area in the image to select yellow as the foreground color.

5. Activate the Flood Fill tool. On the style bar, set Match Mode to None and Fill Style to Solid Color.

6. Click in the selection that you just defined to fill it with yellow.

7. Press Shift+N to remove the selection border.

8. Use the Color Palette to select black as the foreground color.

9. Activate the Paint Brushes tool. On the style bar, select Brush Type: Normal; Size: 10; Shape: Round; Paper Texture: None.

10. Paint in the area under the chin to cover up the corners of the selection that we pasted earlier. At the same time, fill in any white specks that may exist in the back shadow below the mask. When you are finished, the image will look like Figure 11.23.

Figure 11.23 The image after filling in the shadows and retouching the edges of the chin.

All of the preliminary work is done. In fact, preparing the image took most of the effort because the final steps are simple.

1. Select Image|Edge Filters|Trace Contours.
   The result is shown in Figure 11.24.

2. Select Colors|Negative Image. Save the completed image under a new name.

The final image, shown in Figure 11.25, is quite different from the original. It looks more like a neon light sculpture than a photograph. This and other fanciful special effects are among the many possible digital image manipulations.

Figure 11.24 The Trace Contours command emphasizes the edges in the image while removing other details.

Figure 11.25 The final image.

Summing Up

I could easily include a dozen more special effects projects, but I am going to stop here. There is almost no end to what you can do with Paint Shop Pro's special effects tools. I strongly advise you to become familiar with all of the commands, and spend plenty of time experimenting. That special effect you come up with may well be unique, something that nobody has ever seen before.

PART 4

FINAL
TOUCHES

PRINTING YOUR 12 PHOTOGRAPHS

There will come a time when you will want to put your digital image on paper, for anything from a corporate report to a picture of the kids. There are hundreds of reasons why you might want to print your photos. And with today's printing technologies, there are almost as many ways to print images as there are reasons to print them.

There are two approaches to printing: You can do it yourself or you can pay someone to do it. Why would you want to pay to print your photos? It's an unavoidable fact that the types of printers that produce the highest quality prints are rather expensive, and it is a lot easier to justify paying $50 for printing a few photos than it is to spend $5,000 on your own printer. Fortunately, you can get quite good results with much more affordable printers, and the situation will only improve as new printers are introduced.

Printing Technologies

There are three distinct printing technologies that are commonly used in printing digital images: ink jet printers, laser printers, and dye sub printers. Whether you are looking for a printer to purchase for home use, or considering the facilities available at a service bureau, you need to understand how these technologies work and the cost and quality trade-offs involved.

RASTER VS. CONTINUOUS TONE PRINTING

Printing methods fall into two categories: raster and continuous tone. The way raster printers work is similar to the way your computer screen displays pixels. A raster printer creates an image by laying down a grid of dots, with each dot having the color and brightness of the corresponding pixel in the image. When the dots are small enough and close together, they are not visible as individual dots and your eye sees a smooth image. If you take a magnifying glass to a raster image, however, you'll be able to see the dots. Laser and ink jet printers are raster printers.

Continuous tone images are not comprised of dots. Rather, the colors are laid down in a continuous manner much like when you are painting with a brush. Photographic prints and slides made in the traditional manner (with film) are continuous tone, as are prints made with a dye sublimation printer. For photographic images, continuous tone printing methods give the best results.

Ink Jet Printers

If you want a color printer for home use, it will almost surely be an ink jet printer (called *bubble jet* by some manufacturers). Ink jet printers are reasonably priced and can produce surprisingly good color images. An additional advantage is that they can also produce excellent quality monochrome output, which means that you can use the same printer for your photos and for your business letters and similar items.

An ink jet printer works by literally squirting ink onto the paper. The print head contains ink reservoirs that are connected to microscopic nozzles. As the head moves back and forth across the paper, miniscule drops of ink are ejected onto the paper. The size of the drops determines the intensity of the color.

Ink jet printers come in two types: three-color and four-color. Three-color printers fall at the low end of the price scale, and use only the three subtractive primary colors (cyan, magenta, and yellow) to create images. In theory, this should be sufficient because the three primaries combined should produce black. In actuality, however, it is impossible to create a true black in this manner. Output from three-color ink jet printers tends to display black as a dark brown. Some three-color printers let you replace the three-color print head with a black ink monochrome head for printing letters and other text items, but this does not help when you are printing color images, because you cannot print using the three color inks and black ink at the same time.

Four-color ink jet printers solve the problem by adding a fourth color of ink, black, to the print head. In some cases, the black ink is contained in a separate print head, but the two heads—black and color—are used at the same time when printing images. Four-color printers produce markedly better images, and they also avoid the inconvenience of changing print heads when switching from image printing to document printing. If you are considering purchasing an ink jet printer, I highly recommend a four-color model.

Laser Printers

Laser printers have long been the favorite of the business world because of their high-quality output and fast printing. For many years, laser printers printed only monochrome images, but models that print color have recently been introduced. Laser printers are expensive, but their output is very good quality and per-print costs are low.

Laser printers operate similarly to a standard photocopier. A metal cylinder, or *drum*, is treated so that its surface can hold an electrostatic charge. In a photocopier, an image of the original document is focussed onto the drum by means of a lens. This light affects the electrostatic charge so that the charge is stronger where the image is dark and weakest where the image is bright.

In a laser printer, the image is scanned onto the rotating drum by means of a laser and moveable mirrors that are controlled by the data sent from the computer. The result is the same: The electrostatic charge on the drum is a copy of the image.

Next, the drum is exposed to powdered ink, called *toner*. The powder sticks to the drum only where there is an electrostatic charge. The drum is then pressed against the paper and the toner is transferred. Finally, the paper is passed between heated rollers to bind the toner to the paper. In a color laser printer, the principle is the same, but there are three colors of toner and three steps in the process (for the three primary colors).

Dye Sub Printers

Dye sub (for dye sublimation) printers are the Rolls Royces of the color printer world. Dye sub printers produce stunning output that equals or exceeds the quality of the color printing you see in this book or in glossy magazines. They are also very expensive, both for the original purchase and in terms of per-print materials cost.

What makes dye sub printers special is that, unlike ink jet and laser printers, they produce *continuous tone* prints (see the sidebar earlier in this chapter, "Raster Vs. Continuous Tone Printing"). This is accomplished by means of color ribbons (one in each primary color) and a thermal head. As the head moves across the ribbon, it is heated to a degree corresponding to the amount of color required at that location in the image. The heat causes ink in the ribbon to vaporize (sublimate) and be deposited on the paper, where it cools and solidifies. Dye sub printers are slow because three complete scans of the paper, one for each primary color, are required.

While desktop dye sub printers for full size sheets are indeed expensive, there is a new breed of consumer-oriented printer that uses this technology to create photographic print-sized output. These printers are limited to output at 3×5 or 4×6 inches (approximately) but their small size and wide potential market make them quite affordable.

Printing In Paint Shop Pro

There are two parts to printing an image from Paint Shop Pro. First, you must set up the page, specifying the image size and its placement on the page. Then, you must set printer options to control output quality and similar factors. To print an image, you must open it and make sure it is the active image.

Page setup is done in the Page Setup dialog box, shown in Figure 12.1. You display this dialog box by selecting File| Page Setup. Set the options in this dialog box as follows:

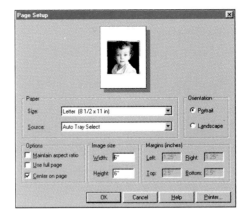

Figure 12.1   The Page Setup dialog box.

- **Paper Size.** Selects the size of paper you will be printing on.

- **Paper Source.** Specifies where the printer gets the paper from. The options available on this list will depend on the printer, as some printers have multiple paper input trays while others have only one. Generally, the Auto Tray Select setting will work if you are using paper in the printer's main input tray. Select Manual Feed if you will be hand-feeding a single sheet to the printer.

- **Orientation.** Specifies if the output will be in Portrait orientation (long edge of paper is vertical) or Landscape orientation (long edge of paper is horizontal).

- **Maintain Aspect Ratio.** If selected, prints the image with its original aspect ratio. If it is off, you can manually set the image width and height independently of each other.

- **Use Full Page.** Prints the image as large as possible on the page.

- **Center On Page.** Centers the image both vertically and horizontally on the page.

- **Image Size.** Specifies the printed image width and height, in inches. If the Maintain Aspect Ratio option is on, changing one of these settings will cause the other to change automatically to maintain the image's aspect ratio.

- **Margins.** Specifies the amount of white space between the image and the page edges. The margins are set automatically and cannot be changed if either the Center On Page or Use Full Page option is selected.

Once you have the page setup options set as desired, click on OK. The image will not be printed yet, but your settings will be remembered.

To print the image, select Print from the File menu, or press Ctrl-P. The Print dialog box will be displayed (Figure 12.2). The settings in this dialog box are:

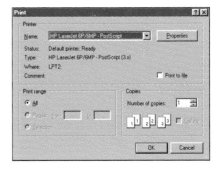

Figure 12.2 The Print dialog box.

- **Printer Name.** Pull down this list and select the printer to use. You will have more than one choice only if you have two or more printers installed on your system.

- **Number Of Copies.** If you want more than one copy of the image printed, enter the number here.

Note that there is a Properties button in the Print dialog box. Clicking this button opens the Properties dialog box for the selected printer. The details of the dialog box are different from each printer, because not all printers have the same options. If your printer has two or more output resolution settings, for example, you will be able to select one in the Properties dialog box. Other settings may include High Quality versus Draft Quality output. You'll also find some settings here, such as Portrait/Landscape orientation, that are also available in the Page Setup dialog box.

Once the printer options are set, click on OK to begin printing.

SAVING PAPER

You certainly don't want to waste any of that expensive ink jet paper, but what if you are printing images that take up only a third or a quarter of a page? Here are two ways to minimize paper waste.

You can create one large image that contains two or more smaller images. Create a new, blank image that will fill an entire page, then copy the smaller images to it and arrange them as desired. After printing the page, use a paper cutter to separate the individual images.

You can also put a single sheet of paper through the printer two or more times. Use Page Setup to set margins so that the first image is printed on the top half of the page. After printing, return the paper to the input tray (be sure the ink has dried) and then print a second image on the bottom half of the page.

Getting The Most From Your Ink Jet Printer

If you will be printing at home, the odds are very good that you will be using an ink jet printer. After all, ink jet printers are reasonably priced, can produce very good looking prints, and can be used for regular text output as well as for your photographs. The first part of this section will help you select an ink jet printer that will meet your needs. Then, I'll present information and tips that will help you obtain the highest possible quality from your printer.

Choosing A Printer

If you're in the market for an ink jet printer, you may be overwhelmed by the huge number of choices. I can't tell you which printer to buy, but I can explain some of the features that you should look at when making a selection.

As explained earlier in the chapter, some ink jet printers use only three colors of ink, while others add black for a total of four colors. I strongly recommend that you get a four-color printer because the image quality is much better. The three-color printers are the least expensive, but getting a 4-color model is a good place to stretch your budget a little if at all possible.

Output resolution is an important specification for any printer, although there is not much difference from one manufacturer to the next. Be sure to check the color printing resolution, as in some models this is lower than the monochrome resolution. For four-color printers, the output resolution ranges from 600×300 to 720×720. Other things being equal, higher resolution is better, but there is no guarantee that a higher resolution printer will create better looking prints. Remember that you do not have to print at the printer's highest resolution, sometimes a lower setting will be just fine. For example, there's no benefit in printing a 300 dpi photograph at 600 dpi.

CARD STOCK

The term *card stock* refers to the thin cardboard that is often used for greeting cards, brochures, and posters. Because it is stiffer than regular paper, some printers cannot handle it properly.

You'll also need to consider paper handling capabilities. Any printer can use regular letter paper, but what about envelopes, transparencies, labels, and card stock? Check the printer's paper path—the route that a sheet of paper travels during printing. Most printers have an L- or U-shaped standard paper path, but many also offer an optional straight path, which does not bend the paper at all. You'll have much more flexibility printing on different kinds of materials if you have the option of using a straight paper path.

Many printer manufacturers are bundling software with their printers. This means that in addition to the basic software required to run the printer, you get one or more additional programs, usually related in some way to imaging and graphics. If the bundled programs are something you'll use, they can add significantly to the value of a printer.

If you plan to do a lot of printing, the cost of consumables is something you need to consider. For an ink jet printer, consumables include the ink cartridges and paper. Color ink cartridges cost in the $20 to $40 range, and the number of pages you can print before having to replace the cartridge determines your average cost per page. Most ink jet printers have a rated "cost per page" that takes these factors into account, and the values I have seen range from 3 1/2 to 20 cents per page. This rating assumes 15 percent color coverage per page, and if you tend to print full color photographs, your cost per page will be higher.

The cost of paper varies quite a bit. You can use standard copier paper that costs less than a penny a sheet, but the results with color images will not be very good. For good quality output, you will have to use special coated ink jet paper that is formulated to absorb the ink in a certain way. This paper can be very expensive, costing up to a dollar a sheet. When considering a specific ink jet printer, you should determine whether it requires a special high price paper for the best results or whether it can use any ink jet paper.

Selecting The Right Paper

Perhaps the most important factor in achieving high-quality output from an ink jet printer is using the right kind of paper. I have already touched on this topic, and I'll provide more information here.

Standard copier paper is inexpensive, but it is designed for photocopiers and laser printers that work by depositing dry ink on the surface of the paper. There is no worry about controlling the way in which liquid ink soaks into the paper. With ink jet printers, however, this is an important factor. You want the ink to soak in a little bit, but not too much or too little. Excessive or insufficient paper absorbancy can have negative effects on image quality. If the ink soaks in too much, it will be hidden inside the paper rather than being visible on the surface. If the ink does not soak in enough, it will spread out on the surface of the paper, resulting in blurring.

Ink jet paper is formulated to have the proper degree of absorbency. Because different manufacturers use different inks, you may get the best results with paper from your printer's manufacturer.

Tailoring Your Image To The Printer

There's no way a printed photograph is going to look exactly like the image on your screen. The two display methods—light emitting phosphors on the screen and light absorbing inks on the print—are so different that an exact match is impossible. There are some things you can do to maximize not only the quality of your prints, but also make them match the screen image as closely as possible.

Working With Gamuts

I have explained previously how the screen display uses additive colors, where the primaries are red, green, and blue, and printing uses subtractive colors, with cyan, magenta, and yellow as the primaries. When you print an RGB image from Paint Shop Pro, color information is automatically converted to CMYK equiva-

WHICH SIDE?

Most ink jet paper has two sides—a right side and a wrong side. To benefit from this special paper, you must print on the correct side. If one side is clearly glossier than the other, that's the correct side. Otherwise, there will be information on the paper box on how to determine which side to print on. Remember that for many ink jet printers, the paper should be placed in the paper tray with the correct side down.

CLEAN YOUR NOZZLES

The ink nozzles on an ink jet printer can become clogged, particularly if the printer is not used regularly. Clogged nozzles usually show up as streaks, mottling, or thin white lines in your prints. Follow the manufacturer's directions for cleaning the ink nozzles in your printer.

GAMUT

The term *gamut* refers to the complete range of colors that can be represented by a particular color model. An out of gamut color is one that cannot be reproduced in the color model being used.

lents by the printer driver before being sent to the printer. However, there is not an exact one-to-one relationship between RGB and CMYK colors. Some colors in the RGB model simply do not exist in the CMYK model. Such colors are called *out of gamut* colors.

What happens when you print an RGB image that contains colors that are out of gamut in the CMYK model? The printer driver converts these colors to the closest CMYK equivalent before sending them to the printer. Generally, these conversions do a pretty good job. An out of gamut red, for example, will be printed as a red, but it will not exactly match the red in the original screen image. RGB colors that are out of the CMYK gamut are some relatively pure, bright primary colors—red, green, and blue.

What can you do about out of gamut colors? With Paint Shop Pro, unfortunately, not much. Paint Shop Pro does not have an on-screen CMYK mode nor does it have a way to identify out of gamut colors in an image. More sophisticated image manipulation programs provide tools to work with gamuts. For example, Adobe Photoshop has an on-screen CMYK preview that temporarily converts the image to CMYK, assigning out of gamut colors the closest CMYK equivalent, then converts it back to RGB mode for screen display. Because the RGB gamut is wider than the CMYK gamut, the CMYK to RGB conversion does not alter any colors, and the result is a screen display that provides a reasonable approximation of what the image will look like when printed.

Photoshop also has a gamut warning that examines an RGB image and then displays in gray all pixels that are out of gamut for the CMYK model. Figure 12.3 shows an example, using an image that was used in one of the book's projects. You can see that almost all of the guard's coat is out of gamut, as well as some other areas of the image. Indeed, the reds in this image are not quite as bright when printed as when viewed on the screen.

Figure 12.3 The original image (left) and displayed with Photoshop's gamut warning (right).

Resolution Issues

When you print an image, you are working with two resolution specifications: the pixel resolution of the image and the output resolution of the printer. Often, these specifications do not match. Let's look at an example.

Suppose that you have an image that is 1000×800 pixels. You want to print it at a size of 5×4 inches on an ink jet printer that has 300 dpi output resolution. The printed image will therefore be 1,500 dots across (5 inches times 300 dots per inch) and 1,200 dots high (4 inches times 300 dots per inch). How is the 1000×800 resolution of the image changed to the 1500×1200 resolution of the output? The answer is that the printer driver software processes the image data to generate the extra needed pixels. If the situation is reversed—the output dimensions are lower than the image dimensions—the printer driver processes the image data to reduce its pixel dimensions.

For the most part, the result of such processing is pretty good. The fact remains, however, that the printed output quality will be highest when there is an exact match between image and printer resolutions. To achieve this, you can resample your image using Paint Shop Pro so that its pixel resolution exactly matches the printer output. Here are the steps required, along with example calculations in parentheses:

1. Determine the output resolution of your printer (300 dpi).

2. Decide on the size that you want the image printed (6×4 inches).

3. Multiply the resolution by the size to calculate the pixel dimensions of the printed image (1800×1200).

4. In Paint Shop Pro, press Shift+S to open the Resample dialog box (Figure 12.4).

5. Turn the Custom Size option on, and turn the Maintain Aspect Ratio option off.

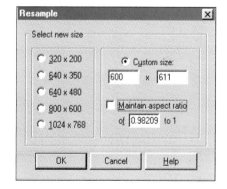

Figure 12.4 You use the Resample dialog box to change an image's pixel dimensions.

6. Enter the dimensions that you calculated in Step 3 in the boxes under the Custom Size option, then click on OK.

7. Print the image. Be sure to use the Page Setup command to specify the image size that you used in your calculations.

Usually there is no reason to save the resampled image because you still have the original image and can resample it again if needed.

This being said, it's true that the printing software usually does a very good job of expanding or contracting an image if needed. You may not notice any improvement from following the steps presented previously, but the only way you will know for sure is to try it on your own system with your own images.

Working With A Print Shop

The alternative to printing images yourself is to use a print shop or service bureau. These establishments will invest in the high-cost printing equipment needed to produce top-quality output, then print your images for a fee. Having some knowledge under your belt can help you get the best service and results from a print shop.

Traditionally, there has been a definite distinction between print shops and service bureaus. Print shops were local firms that specialized in traditional printing, such as business cards, letterheads, and advertising fliers. Service bureaus, on the other hand, were more concerned with providing the pre-press services required by publishers of books and magazines. These distinctions have become somewhat blurred, and the situation is complicated further by the emergence of "copy centers," such as Kinko's, that specialize in photocopying, but may offer other printing services as well. The bottom line is that you cannot be sure who will offer the printing services you need unless you ask.

What exactly do you need to ask before turning your image files over to a shop for printing? Price, delivery time, and satisfaction guarantee are important of course. Here are some other things you should ask about:

- Can you create prints directly from image files on disk?

- What kind of printers do you have?

- What is the maximum printing resolution?

- What image file formats can you use?

- Can I submit my files electronically, via the Internet or email?

- What kinds of paper are available?

If you're lucky, you'll find a local print shop that offers the printing services that you need. If not, you may consider using an *online service bureau*. These bureaus are set up to work at a distance, accepting image files electronically and sending your prints by mail or courier. The disadvantage of using an online bureau is that it is more difficult to work with them to get exactly the results you want, and you cannot examine your prints before they are delivered. They may be your only option, however, particularly if you live in a small town. Start off with a small order to check out the quality of their work and service.

Specialized Techniques

When dealing with printing photographic images, most people tend to think of standard-size prints to put in an album or a frame. With modern techniques, however, there's no reason you need to be limited to standard sizes. In fact, you are not even limited to printing on paper. Some of the possibilities that you may want to explore on your own are:

- Printing transparencies to create a slide show.

- Creating large posters of your images (many service bureaus offer poster-size prints).

- Printing on special thermal paper and transferring your images to T-shirts, coffee mugs—you can even get your photos put on a mouse pad!

- Putting your images on video.

There's a world of possibilities for you to explore. Information on special thermal transfer paper may be provided by your printer manufacturer, and other special techniques are offered by some print shops and service bureaus.

Summing Up

Sometimes, viewing your images on the computer screen just isn't enough. Ink jet printers provide a variety of affordable home-based printing solutions, while print shops and service bureaus provide specialized services that you cannot do yourself. When you have the ability to print your digital images, you'll find uses for them that you never dreamt of before.

DESKTOP
PUBLISHING

13

A few years ago, the term *desktop publishing* was really hot in computer circles. Finally, the power of personal computers and the capabilities of printers had advanced to the point where you could do good quality publishing without ever leaving your desk. Jobs such as brochures, newsletters, and manuals that used to require the services of a professional printing shop could now be done with a PC and a laser printer. Time was saved, money was saved, and everyone was happy—except perhaps the print shop owners!

Once you have collected some digital images of your own, you may want to publish them. What do I mean by "publish?" There's no strict definition, but I am referring to anything in which images and text are combined and printed. There are thousands of possible uses for text and pictures combined, and in this chapter we will work through some projects that will give you an idea of the potential of desktop publishing, as well as introduce some of the most important techniques.

Software For Desktop Publishing

If you look around a software store, you'll find lots of programs that are specialized for desktop publishing (or DTP). You may notice that they all have one thing in common: a high price. Professional DTP programs are highly sophisticated tools with every capability you can think of—and a few you can't—for arranging text and images on a page. Do you need one of these programs to do your own publishing?

Fortunately, the answer is no. Almost every computer user already has at their disposal a program that provides all the DTP power they need: a word processing program. Every word processing program I have seen has the capability to arrange text and images on a page. While word processors lack the high-end tools that dedicated DTP programs offer, they are more than sufficient for beginning to mid-level projects.

MICROSOFT WORD FOR WINDOWS

I have used Microsoft Word 97 for Windows for this chapter's projects. Why did I select this word processing program? There are several reasons:

- It is by far the most popular Windows word processor, and has a much larger market share than its competition. If you have a word processing program, it's likely to be Word.

- It is supplied as a free bonus with many new computer systems. Even if you don't use Word, you are likely to find that any computer you bought within the past couple of years came with Word as a free bonus (or you received the entire Microsoft Office Suite, of which Word is part).

- It is a full-featured word processor with more than enough power to do mid-range DTP.

Even if you do not have Word, don't despair. The word processing program you use almost surely has the tools you need to complete these projects; you'll just have to do some exploring to discover the exact commands that are required. If you have Word for Windows 95, the previous version of Word, you'll find that the commands are almost identical to the new version.

Happy Mother's Day
Creating a photo greeting card

PROJECT 21

Have you priced greeting cards lately? I am amazed at the high prices they are charging for commercial cards. You'll be able to save money as well as provide a more personal greeting if you create your own cards. With a little attention to detail, you can produce cards of such high quality that the recipient will be hard pressed to tell them from the commercial ones.

One limitation when making your own cards is the printing stock—the material the card will be printed on. For a card, you will probably want to use something other than plain paper. Thick paper or card stock (thin cardboard) is appropriate for greeting cards, and you can find both in an array of interesting colors and textures at your local paper specialty shop. Unfortunately, such material is rarely suited for ink jet printing. Even if your printer can handle the thicker-than-normal material, the surface of specialty paper is rarely suited for optimal image reproduction using ink jet printing. The best solution is to use card stock or heavy paper for the main part of the card. Print your images and text on ink jet paper, then cut them out and paste them into the card.

Let's get started. This is a Mother's Day card that I helped my son create. It uses two digital images: a photograph of a rose and a photograph of him in his baseball uniform. We will use the rose for the front cover of the card and the other photo for the inside. Combined with some text, this will make a personal and memorable Mother's Day card that will be much more appreciated than anything bought at the store.

Let's assume that the card will be printed directly on card stock. This introduces some additional complexities because the on-screen elements must be arranged in the precise positions in which they will be printed. If you are printing on regular paper and then cutting out and pasting onto the card stock, you have much more flexibility in positioning things, and therefore, do not have to be so precise when placing on-screen elements. By assuming we are printing directly onto the final card stock you'll learn some of the factors to consider in positioning printed elements on a page.

Think about how things are positioned in a standard greeting card. If you open the card and place it flat on a table, you'll see that the picture on the front of the card is printed on the right half of one side of the paper, and the picture on the inside of the card is printed on the right half of the other side of the paper. This is illustrated in Figure 13.1. Our goal, therefore, is to design two pages that are blank on the left and have the image on the right. We'll print the first image of one side of the paper, and print the second image on the reverse side of the paper. Then, all we need to do is fold the card and we're finished.

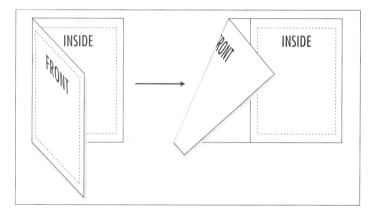

Figure 13.1   The layout of elements for a greeting card.

We want the final card to be 5 inches wide by 6 inches tall. The paper or card stock that we print on will, therefore, need to be 10 inches wide and 6 inches tall. Let's get started. The first task is to define a paper size that is 10" wide and 6" high, with $^1/_2$" margins all around.

1. Start Microsoft Word and click on the New button on the toolbar to create a new, empty document.

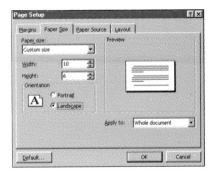

Figure 13.2 Setting a custom paper size in the Paper size dialog box.

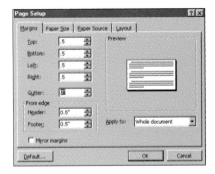

Figure 13.3 Setting the page margins.

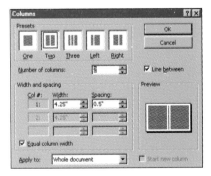

Figure 13.4 The Columns dialog box.

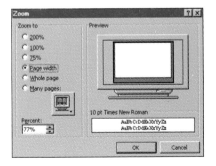

Figure 13.5 The Zoom dialog box.

2. Select Page Setup from the File menu; then, in the dialog box, click the Paper Size tab (Figure 13.2).

3. Under Orientation, select Landscape, then enter 10 in the Width box and 6 in the height box.

4. Click on the Margins tab (Figure 13.3).

5. Enter 0.5 for all four margins: Top, Bottom, Left, and Right.

6. Click on OK.

Next, we will specify that the document has two columns. By leaving the left column empty and putting the image in the right column, we will obtain the arrangement we need. We will also set Word's display mode to make it easier to work, by displaying the document on screen exactly as it will be printed.

1. Select Columns from the Format menu to display the Columns dialog box (Figure 13.4).

2. In the Presets section of the dialog box, click the Two option. This creates two equal-sized columns. Turn on the Line Between option to display a vertical line between the columns.

3. Click on OK.

4. Select Page Layout from the View menu. This puts Word in a display mode where the screen image of your document is essentially an exact replica of what the final printout will look like.

5. Select Zoom from the View menu to display the Zoom dialog box (Figure 13.5). Select the Page Width option then click on OK. This causes Word to scale the display so your whole page is visible on screen.

6. You'll see a blinking vertical line in the top-left corner of the page. This is the *insertion point* where text you type will appear. However, we do not want any text on the left side of the page. Press Enter as many times as needed to move the insertion point to the bottom of the page and then to the top of the second column. You'll see that the line separating the columns appears. Your screen will look like Figure 13.6.

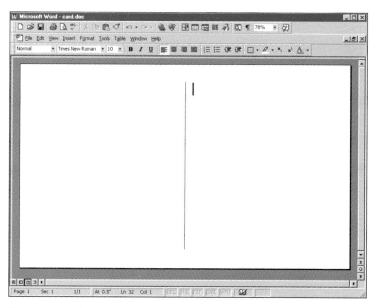

Figure 13.6 The insertion point is positioned at the top of the right column.

Why did we insert a vertical line between the columns? For one thing, it provides us with a visual frame of reference when working in the document. Because it will be included in the printout, it can also serve as a guide for accurately folding the card. If desired, however, we can remove it before printing.

The next step is to insert the image on the front of the card. There will be no text, only a photo.

1. Select Insert|Picture|From File. Word displays the Insert Picture dialog box (Figure 13.7). Find the image file; in this case, the image shown in Figure 13.8. Note how the dialog

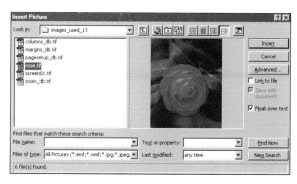

Figure 13.7 The Insert Picture dialog box.

Figure 13.8 This image will be used for the front of the card.

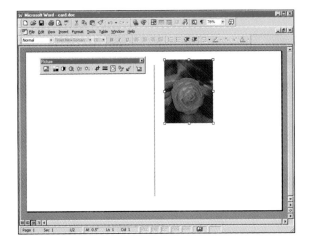

Figure 13.9 After inserting the first image.

Figure 13.10 After adjusting the image size.

box provides a preview of the image file that is highlighted in the file list. If the preview is not displayed, click the Preview button, second from the right at the top of the dialog box. Click on OK when you have the proper image file selected.

2. Word will insert the picture in the document at the location of the insertion point (Figure 13.9). The size that the image is displayed at depends on the image, but you can adjust it as needed. Note that the image has small white boxes, called *handles*, displayed on its edges. Handles are displayed when an image is selected, and are used to change its size.

3. Point at the image with the mouse, noting that the mouse pointer changes to a 4-headed arrow. Drag the picture to the desired location, which in this case is in the center of the right column.

4. Point at one of the image's handles; the mouse pointer changes to a 2-headed arrow. Drag to change the image size.

5. Continue working with the image's position and size until it fills the right column. Click anywhere outside the image to deselect it. Your document will look like Figure 13.10.

6. Use the File, Save command to save the document.

We have completed the first part of the card—the front image. Next, we must do the inside image and text.

CHANGING IMAGE SIZE

If you change an image's size by dragging a corner handle, the image's aspect ratio is preserved. If you drag one of the handles located in the middle of the image's edges, you can change the aspect ratio as you change size.

LINKING IMAGES

When you insert an image using the Insert Picture dialog box, there are two options that determine where the image is stored, and whether the document is updated if the original image file changes. These options are located on the right side of the Insert Picture dialog box (Figure 13.7):

- **Link To File.** When this option is selected, any changes made to the original image file are automatically reflected in the image displayed in your document. If this option is off (the default setting) a copy of the image is stored as part of the document, and changes to the original image file do not affect the document.

- **Save With Document.** This option is relevant only if the Link To File option is selected. If it is on, a copy of the image is stored with the document and is updated if the original image file changes; the copy permits the document to display the image even if the original image file is no longer available. If this option is off, no copy of the image is stored with the document, and the document will display the image only if the original image file is available.

These options involve a trade-off. Storing a copy of images as part of the document results in a large document file, but the document is independent of any other files.

Figure 13.11 The Font dialog box.

Figure 13.12 This image will be used for the inside of the card.

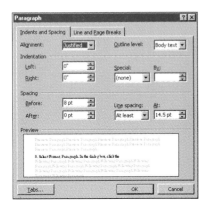

Figure 13.13 Setting the text alignment.

1. Press Ctrl+PgDn to move to the end of the document. Word may have already inserted a second page. If not, press Enter one or more times until a new page is added. Continue pressing enter to move the insertion point to the top of the second column on the second page.

2. Select Format, Font to display the Font dialog box (Figure 13.11).

3. Select the desired font name, style, and size. For the example. I used Monotype Corsiva in Regular style, 28 points. Then click on OK.

4. Type the first part of the message: "Happy Mother's Day," then press Enter.

5. Select Insert|Picture|From File. Insert the image file. For the example, I used the picture shown in Figure 13.12.

6. Use the techniques that you learned earlier to position and size the photograph as desired.

7. Position the insertion point just below the photograph.

8. Select Format, Paragraph. In the dialog box, click the Indents and Spacing tab (Figure 13.13).

9. Open the Alignment list and select Right. This will cause the line of text to align at the right margin of the page.

10. Click on OK.

11. Type the remaining text: "From your Little Slugger." The document will now look like Figure 13.14.

12. Save the document.

We have finished creating the Mother's Day card document, and all that is left is to print it. First, you need to determine how your printer handles the kind of paper or card stock that you are using. Some printers permit you to place it in the standard paper tray, while others require that it be fed manually. Once you have determined this information you can proceed.

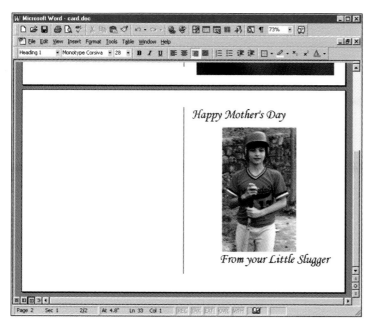

Figure 13.14   The document after adding the second image and text.

1. If your printer does not require manual feed, put the paper in the standard paper tray and proceed to Step 3. Otherwise, select File|Page Setup and click the Paper Source tab (Figure 13.15).

2. Select Manual Feed in both the First Page and Other Pages lists, then click on OK.

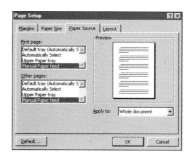

Figure 13.15   Selecting the paper source.

3. If you do not want the vertical line between the columns to print, select Format|Columns to display the Columns dialog box. Turn off the Line Between option and click on OK.

4. Select File|Print to display the Print dialog box (Figure 13.16).

5. Under Page Range, select the Pages option and enter 1 in the adjacent box.

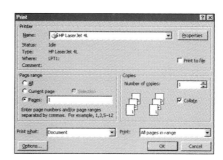

Figure 13.16   The Print dialog box.

6. Click on OK. The first page of the document—the outside image on the card—will be printed. If you are using manual feed, you'll need to feed the paper to the printer.

7. After allowing time for the ink to dry, remove the printout from the printer. Flip it over so the second page will be printed on the reverse side of the paper.

8. Repeat Steps 4 through 6, this time entering 2 as the page to print. The inside part of the card will print.

9. Again, be sure that the ink has dried before handling the printout. Fold the card down the middle, and it is complete. It should look like Figure 13.17. In this figure, the inside and outside of the card have been displayed together.

I think this is a pretty nice card, but we have just started to scratch the surface. The possibilities are almost endless. You could, for example, use Paint Shop Pro to include the card's message as text within an image, or you could add a fancy border to an image before importing it into the document. Whether serious, sentimental, or silly, you can create any kind of card you want.

Figure 13.17 The final Mother's Day card.

PROJECT

22

For Sale By Owner
Create a brochure to advertise your house

Any way you look at it, selling your house is a major undertaking. Everyone wants a quick sale at a good price. If you are selling on your own, without the help of a real estate agent, then it is totally up to you to publicize the house and attract potential buyers. Even if you are using an agent, little extras that you do can make a big difference. One of the most effective things you can do is to prepare a color sales brochure that describes your house and displays photographs of its best features. With a digital camera and a desktop publishing program you have everything you need.

1. Start Word.

2. Select Page Setup from the File menu, and click the Margins tab. You saw this dialog box earlier in Figure 13.3.

3. Set all four margins—Top, Bottom, Left, and Right—to $1/2$ inch. By setting small margins, we have the maximum printable area on our page.

4. Select Format|Font to display the Font dialog box (shown earlier in Figure 13.11). Select a large font for the first line of text. I used Times New Roman in 28 point size.

5. Type in the first line of text (the address and town of the house), then press Enter.

6. Open the Font dialog box again and select a smaller font, such as Times New Roman 14 point. Type in the detail information, using the Tab key to move text toward the right margin and pressing Enter at the end of each line.

MARGINS TOO SMALL?

The minimum margins you can set depend on your printer, because no printer can print all the way to the edge of a page. If you try to set one or more margins that are too small for the currently selected printer, Word will tell you and can also automatically set the smallest margins permitted by the printer.

7. Save the document. At this point the document will look like Figure 13.18.

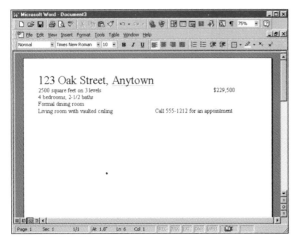

Figure 13.18   The brochure after entering the informational text.

For the remaining steps, we need to have Word's Drawing toolbar available. On all of Word's toolbars, you can determine the function of a button by resting the mouse pointer over it for a moment, without clicking. A *tooltip* will be displayed explaining the button's function.

1. Select Toolbars from the View menu, then select Drawing. Word will display the Drawing toolbar at the bottom of the screen.

2. Click the Line button on the Drawing toolbar. You will use this tool to draw a line under the main line of text.

3. Point at the starting location for the line, under the "123" of the address. Drag to the end position of the line, and release the mouse button. A thin line will be placed in the document. The small white boxes, or handles, at the end of the line indicate that it is selected. If the line's position is

not exactly right, point at one of the handles and drag the end of the line to the desired position.

4. With the line still selected, click the Line Style button on the Drawing toolbar. Word will pop up a menu of available line styles and thicknesses (Figure 13.19).

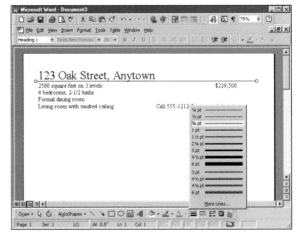

Figure 13.19   Selecting a line thickness/style.

5. Click the desired line style. The line that you just drew will change to the selected style.

The next task is to insert the images in the document, and to add a caption to each image.

1. Press Ctrl+PgDn to move the insertion point to the end of the document.

2. Select Picture from the Insert menu, then select From File. Word displays the Insert Picture dialog box (seen earlier in Figure 13.7).

3. Select the image file that you want to insert, then click on OK. I chose the image shown in Figure 13.20.

Figure 13.20 The first image for the brochure.

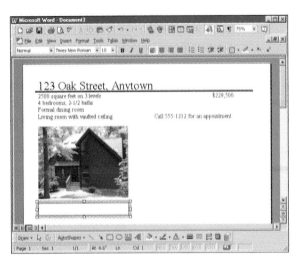

Figure 13.21 After adding a Text Box you are ready to enter the text of the caption.

4. The image is inserted and displayed in the document, with handles around its edges. Use the mouse to position the image (by pointing at the image and dragging) and to adjust its size (by dragging the handles).

5. Click the Text Box button on the Drawing toolbar. We will use this tool to add a caption to the image.

6. Point in the image where you want one corner of the caption to be located, underneath the image that you just added. Drag to the opposite corner and release the mouse button. Word will insert an empty Text Box with a blinking cursor ready for you to enter the caption text (Figure 13.21).

7. Type in the caption text. You do not have to press Enter at the end of each line, as the text will wrap to the next line automatically.

8. Like an image, a Text Box displays handles when it is selected. Use the handles to resize the Text Box if needed. To move a selected Text Box, point at its shaded border and drag.

Repeat these steps to add additional images and captions to the document. Figures 13.22 through 13.24 show the three additional figures that I used in the project. As you add new images, you may find that existing images "hop around" and sometimes are hidden from view as Word tries to fit all the images on the page. You can usually restore things by changing the size of new images, and you can always resort to the Undo command (Ctrl+Z) to reverse your recent actions.

Figure 13.22 A fireplace is always a good selling point.

Figure 13.23   Many potential buyers are attracted by a nice deck.

Figure 13.24   The kitchen is an important feature for many people.

Now add the bulleted list of features at the bottom of the page:

1. Press Ctrl+PgDn to move to the end of the document.

2. Press Enter once to add a blank line between the last image and the new text.

3. Click the Bullets button on the toolbar (this button is on the regular toolbar at the top of the screen).

4. Type in the descriptions of the special features, pressing Enter at the end of each one. Word automatically indents each line and adds a bullet.

5. Save the finished document to disk.

Our final image is shown in Figure 13.25. Of course, your house is not the only thing you can advertise using digital images and DTP. Whether it's a car, a bicycle, or your old Elvis Presley outfit, there's nothing like a color ad with pictures to pull the customers in!

123 Oak Street, Anytown

2500 square feet on 3 levels $229,500
4 bedrooms, 2-1/2 baths
Formal dining room
Living room with vaulted ceiling   Call 555-1212 for an appointment

View from the front yard. The lot is wooded and there is only a small patch of grass to mow.

The rear deck is accessible only from the house and enjoys a natural view.

The living room features a built-in fireplace, vaulted ceiling, and lots of windows.

The newly remodeled kitchen has hand-made Mexican tile and a hardwood floor.

- New roof and gutters in 1996.
- New high-efficiency heat pump with air cleaner installed in 1994.
- Kitchen remodeled in 1995.

Figure 13.25   The final brochure presents the house in an attractive and appealing way.

Summing Up

Desktop publishing, the ability to combine photographs and text in the same document, opens up a whole world of possibilities. You could create an annotated photo album of your son or daughter's birthday party, put together a photo inventory for insurance purposes, or design a brochure that highlights the products that your firm manufactures. If you get serious about DTP, you'll probably want a dedicated DTP program, but as we have seen in this chapter, you can do a lot with your word processing software.

DIGITAL
IMAGES AND
THE WEB

14

One of the most exciting things you can do with your digital images is to put them on your Web pages. There are several things to consider when creating images for the Web. First, Web graphics utilize two special file formats, and you must learn how to choose between these formats for the best result. Second, you need to tailor your images to your online viewers, taking into account the various screen sizes and resolutions that will be used. Finally, you need to add your images, along with text and other elements, to your Web pages. We will cover all of these topics in this chapter.

Web Graphics File Formats

There are literally dozens of different file formats for storing images, but when it comes to Web pages there are only two you need to be concerned with: Graphical Interchange Format (GIF) and Joint Photographic Expert Group (JPEG) format. Let's take a look at each of them.

GIF Files

The GIF file format was developed by CompuServe for transfer of images. Because downloads used to be even slower than they are today, GIF is a *compressed* format in which the data has been processed to result in a smaller file size. It is an 8-bit-per-pixel format, which means that images are limited to a maximum of 256 different colors. Because of this limitation, GIF is not a suitable format for true-color digital images unless you are willing to sacrifice some image quality, but it is ideally suited for limited color images, icons, and the like.

The popularity of the GIF format has received a boost recently due to a few enhancements. One is the *interlaced* GIF specification, which permits the image to be rendered progressively by the Web browser. When you view a non-interlaced image in a browser, it is filled in a line at a time, starting at the top and working down. An interlaced GIF is different. The entire image appears very quickly, but with very little detail. Then, as the remainder of the image is downloaded, the details are progressively filled in. This type of image rendition is much more user-friendly, because it permits the viewers to get an overall idea of the image quickly, then wait for the details only if they are interested.

The second GIF enhancement is the *animated* GIF. I'm sure you have seen these on the Web. They are usually small, animated icons and images. An animated GIF contains several images in a single file. When the images are loaded into a Web browser, the display "flips" through the images in sequence.

Finally, GIF images support a *transparency* option in which one of the image's colors (usually the background color) is transparent and lets whatever is "behind" the image show through. On a Web page, this is usually your background pattern, and using transparency permits an image's main subject to be displayed without a surrounding white (or whatever color the image's background is) rectangle. Figure 14.1 shows the effect of using transparency in a GIF file.

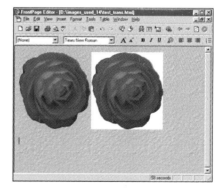

Figure 14.1 A GIF image displayed in a Web page editor with (left) and without (right) transparency.

FILE COMPRESSION

When a file is compressed, its data is processed so that the same data can be stored in a smaller amount of disk space. If you have ever used a ZIP file, you have used file compression. But how is this possible? Won't shrinking the file cause loss of some data?

Data compression works on the principle that much of the information in any data file is redundant. Here's a simple example: Imagine a digital image of a landscape that has a large expanse of blue sky. Many of the pixels in the sky will have the same RGB value. Suppose that the top row of pixels all have the RGB value 10,12,243. If the picture is 500 pixels across, it will take 1,500 bytes to store the data just for that top row of pixels. In a compressed file, however, the same data will be stored as 500,10,12,43 meaning "500 pixels in a row with the RGB value 10,12,243." With two bytes required to store the value 500, and 3 bytes required for the RGB value, we have compressed 1,500 bytes into 5 bytes. This is an oversimplified explanation of how data compression works, but the principle is the same.

There are two general types of data compression. *Lossless* compression retains every single bit of the original data. When the compressed file is decompressed, the result is identical to the original file. *Lossy* compression does not retain all the data, but sacrifices some accuracy to obtain better compression (that is, smaller file sizes). Lossy compression is used primarily with image and sound files, where it has been found that certain parts of the data can be discarded without seriously degrading the image or sound. GIF uses the lossless compression format, while JPEG uses lossy compression.

JPEG Files

The second type of image file that is used on the Web is the JPEG format. The JPEG format uses three bytes per pixel, so it is suitable for true-color images. In fact, some digital cameras use JPEG as the format for downloading images. Like GIF, JPEG is a compressed file format, but it uses a lossy compression scheme. Because the JPEG format was specifically designed for images, the compression method is designed to have the least possible effect on the visual quality of the image.

JPEG supports multiple levels of compression. Almost all programs that support JPEG images, including Paint Shop Pro, let you specify the level of compression to use when saving a JPEG file. Paint Shop Pro uses compression values ranging from 0 to 99. Higher compression values give smaller files, but result in more data loss and, hence, lower-quality images. When working with JPEG images, you can experiment with different compression levels to obtain the best balance between file size and image quality. It is impossible to generalize, because the loss of quality and the file size savings depend on the nature of the image to some extent. Note that the JPEG format supports a *progressive* option, which gives an effect similar to that of interlaced GIF files.

Image Size And Download Time

When you're creating graphics for your Web page, remember that most of the people who view your page will be connected to the Web by a modem. While today's modems are miracles of speed compared to even a few years ago, they are still pretty slow when large graphics files are involved. A 28.8 kilobaud modem operating at maximum speed can transfer a little over 3,000 bytes per second over a clear phone line. That's over a minute— 60 full seconds—to download an uncompressed image that will display at 3×4 inches on the screen! Nobody likes to wait for slow Web pages to display, and the surest way to drive away potential visitors is to have a page that appears on the screen at the speed of a snail.

PNG FORMAT

The newest contestant in the graphics file format battle is Portable Network Graphics, or PNG. It supports 24 bit color, lossless compression, transparency, and interlacing. The main problem is that this format is so new that it has little support at present, but you may see it more often in the future.

Working With GIF Files

You can load a GIF file into Paint Shop Pro and edit it just like any other image. You can also convert images in other formats to the GIF format for use in your Web pages. Remember that GIF is an 8-bit-per-pixel (256 color) format, so images in a 24-bit-per-pixel (true-color) format will have their number of colors reduced when they are converted to GIF. Depending on the nature of the image, this conversion may not give acceptable results. You can check out the effects of color-depth reduction by selecting Colors|Decrease Color Depth, then selecting 256 colors (8 bit) from the next menu. If you like what you see, you can continue with the conversion to GIF. Otherwise, press Ctrl+Z to undo the color-depth reduction.

Before converting an image to GIF format, you may want to reduce its pixel dimensions so the resulting file will be as small as possible. You would use the Resample command to do this. See the section "Optimizing Images For The Web" later in this chapter for more information.

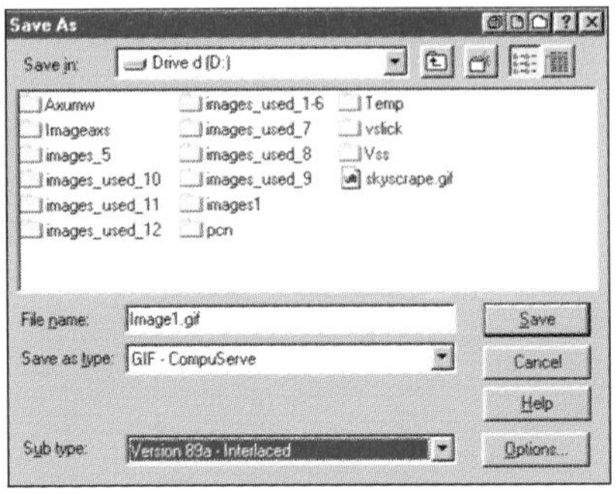

Here are the steps required to save an image in GIF format:

1. Open the image that you want to convert and make it active.

2. Select File|Save As, or press F12, to display the Save As dialog box (see Figure 14.2).

3. Pull down the Save As Type list and select GIF - CompuServe.

4. Pull down the Sub Type list and select Version 89a - Interlaced if you want an interlaced (progressive) GIF file or Version 89a - Noninterlaced if you do not. (The Version 87a selections are for an older GIF format and you can ignore them.)

5. Click the Options button to display the File Preferences dialog box. The GIF tab should already be displayed (Figure 14.3).

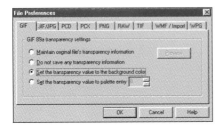

Figure 14.2 Using the Save As dialog box to save a file in a different format.

Figure 14.3 You specify GIF transparency settings in the File Preferences dialog box.

6. Choose a transparency option as follows:

- **Maintain Original File's Transparency Information.**
  Applicable only if the image originated as a GIF file.
  The original file's transparency information (if any)
  is retained.

- **Do Not Save Any Transparency Information.** No transparency information is saved with the file.

- **Set The Transparency Value To The Background Color.**
  The transparent color is set to Paint Shop Pro's current
  background color.

- **Set the Transparency Value To Palette Entry *xx*.** The
  transparent color is set to a specific palette index. Palettes
  are explained later in this chapter.

7. Click on the Preview button to see what the image will look
   like with the selected transparency setting.

8. Enter a name for the file in the File Name box.

9. Click on Save to save the file.

If the image is in true-color mode, Paint Shop Pro will display
a message to the effect that it must be converted to 256 colors
before being saved as a GIF file, and asking you whether to
proceed. You should select Yes.

Working With GIF Palettes

A GIF image, like any 8-bit-per-pixel image, has a *palette*.
A palette is a list of up to 256 different colors that are used in
the image. Each palette entry is a standard RGB color, with red,
green, and blue values in the range 0 to 255. The limitation of
an 8-bit-per-pixel image is not in the range of colors available—
you have the entire spectrum to choose from—but in the number
of different colors in the image. An image of a forest will have a
palette consisting mainly of greens and browns, while an image
of a sunset will have a palette containing mostly reds and oranges.

Figure 14.4 With an 8-bit-per-pixel image, the Eyedropper tool displays the palette index as well as the RGB value.

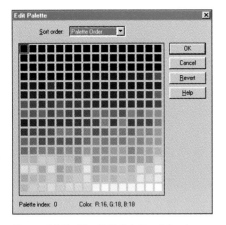

Figure 14.5 The Edit Palette dialog box.

The pixel data in an 8-bit-per-pixel image consists of palette indexes. If a given pixel's value is 188, it means that the pixel is the color that is defined in palette position 188. When you use the Eyedropper tool on an 8-bit-per-pixel image, the Paint Shop Pro Color Palette displays not only the RGB value of the pixel you are pointing at, but also its palette index. This is shown in Figure 14.4. This figure indicates that the Eyedropper tool is pointing at a pixel whose data value is 32, and that palette entry 32 has the RGB value 131, 110, 84.

The way that paletted images work means that you can change an image's colors without modifying its pixel data at all—all you need do is change its palette. To edit a palette, do the following:

1. Load the image whose palette you want to edit. Only 256 color images, such as GIF format, have palettes; you cannot edit the palette on, for example, a JPEG image because it doesn't have one.

2. Press Shift+P, or select Colors|Edit Palette, to open the Edit Palette dialog box (see Figure 14.5).

3. The dialog box displays the 256 palette entries in a 16×16 grid of small boxes. The selected color is indicated by a black border around it, and the selected color's palette index and RGB value are displayed at the bottom of the dialog box. Click any color to select it.

4. Open the Sort Order list at the top of the dialog box and select how the palette entries are sorted in the dialog box display with one of the following entries:

   • **Palette Order**. Entries are sorted by their palette index, starting at 0.

   • **By Luminance**. Entries are sorted from brightest to darkest.

   • **By Hue**. Entries are sorted according to their position on the standard color wheel. The order is reds, purples, blues, greens, yellows, browns, and grays.

5. Double-click on a palette entry to edit it. Paint Shop Pro will open the Color dialog box (see Figure 14.6).

6. Select the new color in one of the following ways:

   - If the desired color is displayed in the Basic Colors grid, click on it.

   - Enter the desired RGB values in the Red, Green, and Blue boxes.

   - Click on the desired color in the large color selection rectangle, then adjust its brightness using the slider bar at the right of the dialog box.

7. When you have selected the desired color in the Color dialog box, click on OK. You will return to the Edit Palette dialog box. The selected palette entry will now reflect the new color.

8. Repeat Steps 5 through 7, as needed, to edit additional palette entries.

9. At any time, click on the Revert button to discard all your editing changes and return the palette to its original state.

10. When finished, click on OK to save the edited palette and apply it to the image.

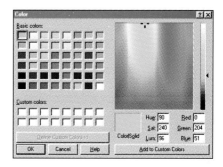

Figure 14.6 You edit a color in the Color dialog box.

Why would you want to edit an image's palette? One reason is to modify colors in an image that would be difficult or impossible to change using Paint Shop Pro's Red/Green/Blue dialog box. For example, suppose you have a photograph of an apple tree with several dozen red apples hanging on it. You want to increase the intensity and brightness of the red color of the apples. It would be a next-to-impossible task to individually select each apple. By editing the image palette, however, you can brighten all the reds in the palette and the changes will be applied just to the apples (assuming they are the only red things in the image).

Working With JPEG Files

Converting digital photographs to JPEG format for use on the Web is a simple process, because JPEG is a 24-bit-per-pixel format and you do not need to worry about reducing color depth, palettes, and so on. The only choice you need to make is the degree of compression. Here are the steps to follow:

1. Open the image you want to convert.

2. Select File|Save As, or press F12, to open the Save As dialog box (shown earlier in Figure 14.2).

3. Open the Save As Type list and select JPG - JPEG -JFIF Compliant.

4. Open the Sub Type list and select either Progressive Encoding (for an image that is rendered progressively) or Standard Encoding (for non-progressive rendering).

5. Click on the Options button to display the File Preferences dialog box. Enter the desired compression value in the box, then click on OK to return to the Save As dialog box.

6. In the Save As dialog box, enter the desired file name in the File Name box.

7. Click on Save.

Optimizing Images For The Web

When you are preparing one or more images for use on the Web, it is worth your while to spend some time optimizing them for Web use. This is particularly true if your Web pages include a lot of images, and the images are an important component of your pages rather than merely being decorative. The discussion in this section applies to true-color digital photographs, and is not necessarily relevant to other kinds of images, such as icons, logos, and graphical text.

An important choice is whether the image should be in GIF or JPEG format. GIF files are a lot smaller, because they devote only one byte (as compared with JPEG's three bytes) to store each

CONSIDER YOUR VIEWERS

When designing Web pages, it is essential to remember that your pages will be viewed by all kinds of people who are using different types of systems. Most important is the fact that screen sizes and resolutions differ. Some people are using a 14-inch monitor at 640×480 resolution, while others may have a 21-inch screen at 1600×1200. There are a lot of possibilities between these extremes, too. A lot of the dimensions that you set when creating a Web page, such as the display size for images, are specified in pixels. A 400×300 pixel image may look fine on your big screen, but when someone with a 14-inch monitor views the page, it will be too big.

It's a good idea to design your pages with the least common denominator in mind. This means designing your pages to fit a 640×480 screen size. Someone using this screen resolution should be able to view your page without problems or inconveniences, such as having to scroll horizontally to see everything. The next step up in screen resolution, 800×600, is probably available to 95 percent of viewers, so it might be a reasonable compromise between the lowest screen resolution and some of the higher resolutions. If you have a larger screen, set your browser or page design software to a partial screen window that has pixel dimensions approximately equal to the smallest size for which you are designing. For example, if your screen is 1280×960 and you are designing for 640×480, set your window to half the screen's height and width. Then you'll be sure that the pages you design will be easily viewable by people with lower resolution monitors.

pixel. Their limited color depth, however, makes them unsuitable for some images. For true-color digital photographs, I feel that JPEG is always preferable in terms of image quality. If file size is a pressing concern for you, it may be possible to convert some photographs to GIF format with acceptable final quality. Only you can be the judge.

If you have decided to use JPEG format for your photographs, the next decision you must make is the level of compression to use. As I mentioned previously, I feel that a compression level of 15 is a good choice, which provides a significant savings in file size with minimum impact on image quality. Again, however, you should judge for yourself. Save five versions of your image with compression levels of 5, 10, 15, 20, and 25. View them in your browser and see how they compare, then check the file sizes and make a decision.

It is also important to optimize the image size. This means that the image's pixel dimensions should be exactly the same as they will be when the image is displayed on your Web page. Thus, if during page design you decide that a particular image should be displayed at 200×150 pixels, then that is the optimum size for the image. Other sizes are undesirable:

- If the image's pixel dimensions are larger than the image's display size, the extra pixels will be wasted and you'll have a larger file with no improvement in display quality.

- If the image's pixel dimensions are smaller than the image's display size, the browser will "stretch" the image to fit, and the display quality will be reduced.

When designing your page, the image's pixel dimensions do not matter because your browser or page design program will stretch or shrink the image to fit the specified size. Once you have settled on a display size, that's the time to use Paint Shop Pro's Resample command to change the image's pixel dimensions by doing the following:

1. Press Shift+S, or select Image|Resample, to display the Resample dialog box (see Figure 14.7).

2. Turn the Maintain Aspect Ratio option off.

3. Be sure that the Custom Size option is turned on, and enter the image display dimensions in the two boxes under it.

4. Click on OK.

5. Save the resampled image under a new name.

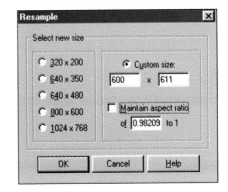

Figure 14.7 You use the Resample dialog box to change an image's pixel dimensions.

Despite the instruction given in Step 2, I think it is generally preferable to maintain an image's original aspect ratio—its width/height proportion—when changing its pixel dimensions. Some images, although not all, do not look right when their aspect ratio is changed. To maintain the aspect ratio, use your Web page design program to determine the exact display width, accepting an approximate value for the height. Then, do the following:

1. Press Shift+S, or select Image|Resample, to display the Resample dialog box.

2. Turn the Maintain Aspect Ratio option on.

3. Be sure that the Custom Size option is turned on, and enter the image width in the first of the two boxes under it. Paint Shop Pro will automatically calculate the proper height; make a note of this value.

4. Click on OK.

5. Save the resampled image under a new name.

6. Go back to your Web page design program and enter the image height that Paint Shop Pro calculated.

Adding Images To Your Pages

How do you insert an image into your Web page? This is not the place for a complete treatment of Web page authoring, but I can cover a few image-related basics. There are plenty of good books available on this subject.

DISPLAYING LARGE IMAGES

If you need to display several large images on
your Web page, there's an approach that can save
your viewers the time of downloading images they
don't want to see. Save two versions of each image: a full size, high-quality copy and a small,
lower quality copy. Create an "index" page on
your Web site that displays the smaller images,
with each small image being a link to the full size
version. This permits users to download and view
only the large images they are interested in. You
can see a beautiful example of this approach
at www.kodak.com/digitalImages/samples/
majesticPix.shtml.

All Web pages are text documents written in HTML, which stands for *Hypertext Markup Language*. The text in an HTML document consists almost entirely of two things:

- Text that is actually displayed when the document is viewed in a browser, such as Netscape Navigator or Microsoft Internet Explorer.

- Special codes that provide instructions for the browser, such as how to format text, links to other pages, and what images to display. HTML codes are always enclosed in brackets **<like this>**.

Details of inserting image codes in your HTML documents differ from one page editor to another, with the process being partially automated in most cases. This means that instead of typing the codes in directly, you make selections and entries in a dialog box and the program generates the HTML code automatically. Knowing the details of the codes, however, will enable you to fine-tune your pages as needed.

The basic code to display an image code is this

```
<IMG SRC=filename>
```

where *filename* is the name of the image file. Practically, however, the minimal image tag has two additional elements, or attributes:

```
<IMG SRC=filename HEIGHT=xxx WIDTH=yyy>
```

In this code, the **HEIGHT** and **WIDTH** attributes specify the size, in pixels, at which the image is to be displayed. If these are omitted, the image will be displayed at its own pixel dimensions, which is usually exactly what you want. There are two advantages, however, to specifying the **HEIGHT** and **WIDTH** attributes in an **<IMG>** tag:

1. You can specify a display size that is different from the image's own pixel dimensions.

2. Knowing the image's display size, the browser can reserve space for it and continue displaying text and other elements while the image downloads. Otherwise, the browser must wait for the entire image to download before it can determine its size.

HTML defines several other optional attributes for an <IMG> tag:

- **ALIGN**. Specifies how surrounding text is aligned with respect to the image. Permitted settings include **LEFT**, **RIGHT**, **TOP**, **BOTTOM**, and **MIDDLE**.

- **ALT**. Defines the text that will be displayed in place of the image, either while the image is loading or if the image is not available for some reason.

- **BORDER**. Gives the thickness, in pixels, of the border surrounding the image. If you don't want a border, set **BORDER** to 0.

- **HSPACE**. Defines the space, in pixels, between the left and right edges of the image and surrounding text.

- **VSPACE**. Defines the space, in pixels, between the top and bottom edges of the image and surrounding text.

Here's an example of an HTML <IMG> tag that uses all of these attributes:

```
<IMG SRC="waterfall.jpg" HEIGHT=400 WIDTH=275
ALT="Waterfall image"
BORDER=0 HSPACE=10 VSPACE=10 ALIGN=RIGHT>
```

Note that progressive rendering of GIF and JPEG images, as well as transparency in GIF images, is defined within the image file itself and does not have to be specified in the HTML tag.

Summing Up

By following the tips and techniques I have presented here, you will be able to put your digital photos on the Web with the best image quality and smallest files possible. Choice of image file type and use of the optimal image size are the two most important factors that influence the appearance and download time of your Web images. And just like that old beer commercial slogan "tastes great, less filling," you want your Web pages to "look great, download fast."

APPENDIX:
PAINT SHOP

The one essential tool for working with digital images is a program that lets you manipulate your photographs. There are several excellent programs of this type, such as Adobe PhotoShop and Corel PhotoPaint, and if you like, you can run down to your local computer store and plunk down several hundred dollars for one of these commercial programs. Fortunately, you don't need to because this book's CD-ROM contains an excellent image manipulation program called Paint Shop Pro.

How can we provide such a powerful program for free? The answer is that Paint Shop Pro is *shareware*, a method of software distribution that lets you try before you buy. You can use the program for 30 days and see if you like it and determine if it's something you will continue to use. Then, and only then, are you asked to register the program and pay for it. If you do not like the program, you are under no obligation to buy. Of course, no one can force you to pay—you can keep using the evaluation version for ever. But the price ($69.00) is so reasonable compared with commercial programs, it's affordable to be honest. I hope that your sense of fair play would play a role too!

How does Paint Shop Pro compare with commercial image manipulation programs such as PhotoShop? To be honest, it is not quite their equal. Of course, a Toyota Camry is not the equal of a Mercedes 500SL—but it still is an excellent car for 99.9 percent of drivers. The same is true of Paint Shop Pro. It is more than adequate for all of the projects in this book, and is likely to meet all of your digital image manipulation needs for a long time to come.

Throughout this book, I provide detailed instructions on how to use Paint Shop Pro to complete the various projects. Before you get started, however, it's a good idea to have a general idea of how the program operates. In this appendix, I explain the fundamentals of using Paint Shop Pro. If you have some experience with Windows programs, you may not need this, or may only need certain sections for reference.

Please note that the following is a brief explanation of the basics, and is by no means a complete description of all the program's features. My goal is to teach you the minimum you need to get started using the program.

Windows Basics

Like all Windows programs, Paint Shop Pro displays information (including images) in windows. Likewise, you tell the program what to do by means of menus, commands, and dialog boxes.

Using Menus

The menu bar across the top of the screen displays the menu commands. Each of these commands leads to a menu that, in turn contains additional commands. Related commands are grouped together; for example, file related commands are on the File menu. To select a menu command, you can use either the mouse or the keyboard:

- With the mouse, click on the desired command on the menu bar, then click on the desired choice on the pull-down menu.

- With the keyboard, press and hold the Alt key, then press the key corresponding to the underlined letter in the menu command. For example, press Alt+F to open the File menu. Then, press the key corresponding to the underlined letter shown in the pull-down menu.

Some menu commands carry out a program action immediately. Other commands display a submenu, from which you select the final command as described above. Still other commands display a dialog box, which is explained next.

Dialog Boxes

When Paint Shop Pro needs some additional information from you in order to carry out an action, it displays a dialog box. There are dozens of different dialog boxes, and each one is unique, but they all use the same few elements in different combinations. These elements are illustrated in Figure A.1 and explained as follows:

SHORTCUT KEYS

Some of the more commonly used menu commands are assigned shortcut keys. Pressing the shortcut key has the same effect as selecting the command from the menu. For example, Ctrl+O is the shortcut key for the File|Open command. Shortcut keys are listed next to the associated command on the menu.

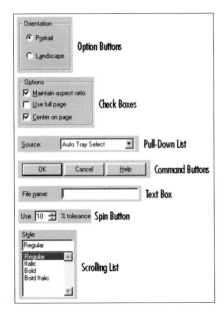

Figure A.1 Dialog box elements.

- **Option Buttons**. Select one and only one option in the group.

- **Check Boxes**. Select any number of options.

- **Text Box**. Type in or edit text.

- **Scrolling List**. Select an item from the list.

- **Pull-Down List**. Click the down arrow to display the list, then select an item.

- **Spin Button**. Type in a number, or click the up or down arrow to change the value.

- **Command Buttons**. Click to carry out an action. OK accepts the dialog box entries, closes the dialog box, and executes the associated action. Cancel closes the dialog box without executing the associated action. Help displays information related to the dialog box.

To work in a dialog box, select the element you want to change either by clicking it or by pressing Alt plus the letter that is underlined in the item's caption. You can also move forward or backward from item to item by pressing Tab and Alt+Tab.

Working With Windows

The Paint Shop Pro program runs in its own window. Within the Paint Shop Pro window, each image that you load is displayed in its own sub-window within the Paint Shop Pro main window. The main Paint Shop Pro window also contains several other items, as described here and illustrated in Figure A.2.

- The menu bar displays the menu commands.

- The Toolbar displays icons you can click to carry out certain commands. Rest the mouse pointer over a toolbar button for a moment and Paint Shop Pro Help will display the button's name.

- The Status Bar displays information related to your current activity.

- The Color Palette and other special elements can be displayed or hidden as needed using the View menu.

- The Style Bar displays options for the active tool.

ENTER AND ESCAPE

In most dialog boxes, pressing Enter is the same as clicking on the OK button, and pressing Esc is the same as clicking on the Cancel button. In some dialog boxes the "do it" button is not labeled "OK" but has another label related to the function of the dialog box—for example, "Save."

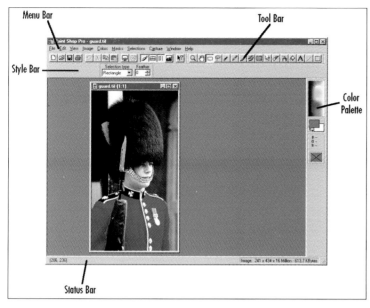

Figure A.2   Elements of the Paint Shop Pro screen.

You can control which of these elements is displayed by selecting the item from the View menu.

Every window has a title bar across the top that displays the name of the window. Only one window at a time can be *active*. The active window has a dark title bar, while inactive windows have gray title bars. To make a window active, click anywhere in the window. You can also open the Window menu and select the desired window from the list.

When a window is *restored*—not at its maximum size—you can move it by pointing at the title bar and dragging to the new location and you can also change its size by pointing at its border and dragging. Restored is one of the following three states that an open window can be in:

- **Minimized**. The window is displayed as a small icon at the bottom of the screen.

- **Maximized**. The window is at its maximum size. For the Paint Shop Pro program window, this is the entire screen. For an image window within Paint Shop Pro, this is the full area within the Paint Shop Pro program window.

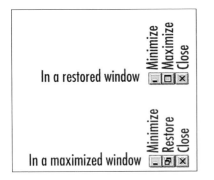

Figure A.3   Control buttons displayed on a maximized or restored window.

- **Restored**. The window is displayed at an intermediate size—it does not fill the whole screen

When a window is maximized or restored, it displays three buttons in the top right corner that you click to change the window state, as shown in Figure A.3. When a window is minimized, its icon displays Restore, Maximize, and Close buttons. Clicking a window's Close button is the same as selecting File|Close when the window is active.

You'll note that the title bar of most windows has three buttons at its right end. You use these as follows:

- **Close button**. Click this button (on the right with the "X") to close the window. If you close the main Paint Shop Pro window the program will terminate.

- **Minimize button**. Click this button (on the left with the horizontal line) to reduce the window to a small icon. If you minimize an image window, the icon displays at the bottom of the Paint Shop Pro window, and can be restored by clicking the icon and then clicking Restore in the menu that displays. If you minimize the main Paint Shop Pro window the icon displays on your Windows taskbar and can be restored by simply clicking the icon.

- **Restore button**. Click this button (the one in the middle) to switch the window to its maximum size or back to an intermediate size.

When a window is at an intermediate size you can fine-tune its dimensions by pointing at the border of the window and dragging to the new size.

Opening, Saving, And Converting Files

Images that you work with in Paint Shop Pro are saved in disk files. Each file has a specific name that is assigned when the file is created, and also a format that determines how the image data is stored in the file. Opening, saving, and converting image files are an important part of working in Paint Shop Pro.

MOUSE TERMINOLOGY

If you're new to computers, you may not be familiar with using the mouse. Here's what you need to know:

- **Click.** Move the mouse pointer over a specific item on the screen and quickly press and release the left mouse button.

- **Right-click.** The same as click, but use the right mouse button.

- **Double-click.** The same as click, but press and release the mouse button twice.

- **Drag.** Point at a screen object, then press and hold the left mouse button. Move the mouse pointer to the new location and release the mouse button.

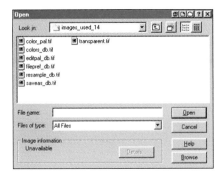

Figure A.4 The Open dialog box.

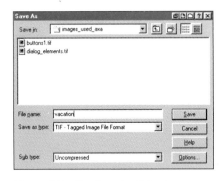

Figure A.5 The Save As dialog box.

Opening An Image

You can open any image that is present on your disk. Once it is open, you can edit it, print it, and so on. To open an image from disk:

1. Press Ctrl+O or select File|Open to display the Open dialog box (Figure A.4).

2. The dialog box will list all of the image files in the current folder. To look in a different location, open the Look In list and select the desired folder.

3. Click on the name of the desired file to select it. Or, you can type the file's name into the File Name box.

4. Click on Open.

The selected image will be opened and displayed in its own window. The image's file name will be displayed in the window's title bar.

Saving An Unnamed Image

If you are working on a new image, one that you created from scratch or read in from a scanner, for example, you must assign it a name and decide on a file format when you save it to disk. New images are assigned default names of the form Image1, Image2 in Paint Shop Pro, but you should assign more meaningful names when you save them. Here are the steps required:

1. Select File|Save As or press F12 to display the Save As dialog box (Figure A.5).

2. If necessary, open the Save In list to select the folder where you want the image saved.

3. Open the Save As Type list and select the file format you want the image saved in.

4. Type the file name in the File Name box. Paint Shop Pro will automatically add the appropriate extension for the file format that you selected.

5. Click on Save.

If the folder already contains an image file with the name that you specified, Paint Shop Pro will display a dialog box asking if you want to replace the old file. You have two choices:

- **Yes**. The new image file will overwrite the old one.

- **No**. You will be returned to the Save As dialog box where you can specify either a different folder or a different file name.

Saving A Named Image

If an image already has a name (as displayed in its title bar) you must save it in order to retain changes made while editing the image. You can tell that an image has been modified because an asterisk is displayed next to its name in the title bar. You may also want to save the image with a different name. This is useful when you want to retain both the original version of the image and the edited version. Use one of the following methods when saving an image:

- To save an image with its original name, press Ctrl+S.

- To save an image with a new name, press F12 to display the Save As dialog box (Figure A.5). Enter the new name in the File Name box, then click on Save.

Converting An Image To A Different Format

There will be times when you want to convert an image from one file format to another. For example, to be used on the Web, a file must be in either GIF or JPEG format (as explained in Chapter 14). Here's how to convert a file to a different format:

1. Open the image file in Paint Shop Pro.

2. Press F12 to display the Save As dialog box (Figure A.5).

3. Open the Save as Type pull-down list and select the desired image file format.

4. If you want the file to have a new name, enter it in the File Name box. This step is optional.

5. Click on Save.

You can, but do not have to, assign a new name to the converted file. This is because Paint Shop Pro will automatically add a different extension to the file name, the extension that is associated with the specified file format. For example, if you open a file in TIFF format named ROVER.TIF and use the previous steps to convert it to GIF format, Paint Shop Pro will save it as ROVER.GIF.

Working With Selections

One of the most important tools in Paint Shop Pro is the ability to *select* part of an image. When an image has a selection defined, any editing actions that you take affect only the part of the image within the selection; other parts of the image are unaffected. You can also delete a selection, and you can copy or move it to another location in the image or to an entirely new image. When an image has a selection defined, the border of the selection is marked by a blinking dashed line.

When you create a selection, you also specify the degree of *feathering*. When feathering is set to 0, the selection has sharp edges. Higher levels of feathering give progressively softer edges, as shown in Figure A.6.

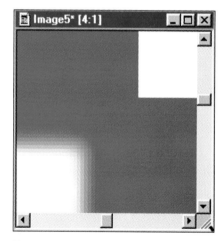

Figure A.6 A rectangle created with no feathering (right) and with maximum feathering (left).

There are two ways to manually define a selection:

- **Geometrical shapes**. Activate the Selection tool by clicking the toolbar button that has a dotted rectangle on it. Select the desired shape and feather setting on the Style bar, then drag in the image to define the selection. You can select an area that is a rectangle, square, circle, or ellipse.

- **Freehand**. Activate the Freehand tool by clicking the "lasso" button on the toolbar. Set the feather level on the Style bar. Drag in the image to draw the selection boundaries.

The third method of defining a selection is automatic—it will create a selection that includes areas of the image that are "similar" in brightness and color to the area clicked on. This is done with the Magic Wand tool. Chapter 4 explains how to use it.

Using any of these selection tools, you can define a selection that includes two or more areas of the image that are not connected to each other. To do so, define the first area, then hold down the Shift key while defining the other areas.

While a selection is defined:

- Press Shift+N to remove the selection definition.
- Press Shift+V to invert the selection. The new selection will include all areas that were previously unselected.

INDEX

771.32/AiT

WHAT'S ON THE CD-ROM

The *Digital Camera Design Guide* CD-ROM contains a variety of programs that you may find useful when working with your digital images. There is also an installation program that you can use to install the various programs onto your hard disk. Here's what you'll get:

- Paint Shop Pro, the full-featured image manipulation program that is used in the book's projects.

- ImageAXS, a useful image cataloging program to keep track of your images.

- GIF Animator, to create animated GIF files for use on the Web.

- Photo Album, to organize your images.

- PhotoImpact and PhotoExpress, two more fun programs for image manipulation.

- The CoffeeCup HTML editor for creating Web pages.

- A selection of images from the book. You can use these images to work through the book's projects, for further creative explorations, and in your own non-commercial publishing projects.

See the *readme* files in each folder for acknowledgments, descriptions, copyrights, installation instructions, limitations, and other important information.

Requirements

The shareware tools are platform-specific to Microsoft Windows 3.1 or Microsoft Windows 95.